Bootle

CW01082394

Bred

Growing up in Bootle in the 50s
and 60s

This book is dedicated to the memory of

Jack, Norman, John and Kenny four of the finest that Bootle (and Litherland) has ever produced.

Contents

Foreword

The events and places in this book are as I remember them over fifty years ago, but memory is fallible and if there are mistakes then they are all mine and I apologise for them. In most cases I have used real names, and I hope the people I have referred to are not offended as I remember them with great affection, but I have changed some for reasons of sensitivity. Bootle was, and is, a very special place and those who, like me, were raised there never fail to speak of it with pride and a real warmth. I do not subscribe to the view that things were always better in the past, and certainly aspects of life were difficult and challenging, but in my case, and I am sure for many others, it was a wonderful time to be growing up and a great place in which to be doing it. Hopefully the book will stir some happy memories for you as it did for me in writing it.

Chapter One Beginnings

"I was born by the river in a little tent," Sam Cooke

I wasn't born in a tent like Sam Cooke, but I was born by the river, the River Mersey that is, in Wordsworth Street off Marsh Lane, down by the docks. My street had been heavily bombed during the Blitz and like most of Bootle was just beginning to recover from the devastating results of the Luftwaffe's campaign of aerial bombardment in trying to destroy the country's main source of supply and vital supplies to maintain the war effort. Liverpool and Bootle docks had become essential to Britain during the Battle of the Atlantic, the longest battle of the war and the convoys were controlled from an underground command centre, the "Western Approaches", below Derby House in the city centre. This is now a museum and a very interesting place to visit. The food, fuel and troops that came through the port saved Britain and were critical in contributing to the plans for the liberation of Europe. In the May Blitz of 1941, over seven consecutive nights, German bombers dropped 870 tonnes of high explosive bombs on Merseyside and over 112,000 incendiary bombs starting fires all over the city. Many of these were targeted on Bootle docks and surrounding areas causing extensive damage, injuries and death. It is estimated that only ten per cent of properties in Bootle were left unscathed and 409 people were killed. Altogether this made the borough the hardest hit per capita in the country and through it all the only protection was from ground based anti-aircraft ordinance, the Prime Minister Winston Churchill deciding to reserve the RAF fighters for the defence of the capital. Despite their role in what became known as the "Forgotten Blitz" the people of Bootle were nothing if not resilient and stoic. Britain may have won the war but it did not always feel like that as people continued to live amongst the rubble of bomb damage and still had to cope with the post war austerity and rationing, which continued until 1954. When I was young the war was still very much part of the narrative when people got together and I remember my Mum describing how at night her family, like many others, gathered around the wireless to listen to the broadcasts of Lord Haw Haw, so named because of his posh accent, (this was officially discouraged by the government) who tried his best to weaken the morale of the people but in fact had the opposite effect and he was regarded as a figure of ridicule. On one occasion he chillingly named her street in a list of areas which were to be targeted that evening and he said that "the kisses on your windows won't help you," referring to the tape fixed in x shapes on windows to prevent flying glass. His real name was William Joyce, and he was an American-born Briton who became a member of Oswald Mosley's British Union of Fascists. Before war was declared in 1939, he fled to Germany and became a naturalised German citizen in 1940. Joyce was captured in Germany at the end of the war, tried and found guilty of treason. This was controversial as he was born in the USA to Irish parents and he had American and German nationality, but there was little sympathy for him in this country. He was hanged by Albert Pierrepoint and remains the last person to be executed for treason in Britain.

So, I grew up in a terraced street which had several prefabricated houses built on both sides of the middle of the street, as a constant reminder of the result of a particular bombing pattern and where the adults often talked of their war experiences and the people who had not survived. One of our neighbours recalled her elderly mother who refused to sit in the street's air raid shelter but instead would often stand outside brandishing her sweeping brush as a weapon and cursing the German bombers overhead with every profanity she knew, and her knowledge was pretty extensive by all accounts. I often think that the Germans, who had not met this particular lady or my Gran for that matter, could not have realised what was waiting for them if they had invaded Britain. The war experience helped to reinforce the great community spirit which already existed in the working-class streets at that time when people supported one another, and help was always close at hand. Although I was not a war baby, the war and its aftereffects still featured strongly in my consciousness as I grew into childhood. Years later I took my children to a special Blitz Exhibition in the Liverpool Museum. It was fascinating with all sorts of exhibits including the wheel of a bomber which had crashed to the ground and incendiaries that had failed to ignite. What really caught my attention though was a series of photographs from a German daylight reconnaissance plane picking out targets for the bombers. My Dad was a dock gateman and had worked on the docks throughout the war. There was a small hut on Gladstone Dock that he could use. I visited it many times as I was growing up. It had a small bunk, table and chairs and a small stove. There on one of the Luftwaffe photos taken from high in the air was a picture of Gladstone Dock with a target cross centred on my Dad's hut! I was outraged and blurted out, "They were trying to bomb my Dad!" It left me with a sense of how real the danger was for those who had lived through those times and an affinity for a war I had not experienced but still felt connected to.

I came into the world on a very cold, November day in 1952. I was the youngest of three children with an older brother John, who was a war baby, and a sister Tricia eighteen months my senior. According to family gossip I picked up in the following years, I suspect that I was a bit of a surprise and that my parents were content with the set they already had of a boy and girl. I was delivered at home in the front parlour, one of the very few occasions I was allowed in there, it being a room kept for special occasions. My Gran was the only other person present to help my mother as she delivered all the babies in the family at that time - no midwives or fancy nursing homes for us. In fact, my mother had never attended any prenatal classes or the GP's for that matter. I find this strange as the NHS had been launched four years before in 1948 and my mother would have had access to those services but tradition is everything and in some ways we lived in a bubble which was more representative of the 1930's or even earlier and the Marsh Lane area often seemed to me, looking back, to have much of the features of the Irish towns and villages that many of the people's parents and grandparents had originated from. Apparently, I spent the first few nights of my life sleeping with my Gran, when not requiring a feed, to let my Mum rest. I must have been quite a tough baby to survive this experience as my Gran was quite a character and liked a drink. After that I was moved to my parents' bedroom and slept in a drawer lined with blankets. No expensive swinging cot for me. I remember very little of my first few years and there are very few pictures of me as a child. This was not unusual. At the time many families did not own a camera and if they did then it was used sparingly as film and developing costs were relatively expensive. This was in the days when the roll of film had to be extracted from the camera carefully in a darkened room and taken to the chemists to be developed. There was then a fairly long wait before the pictures could be collected and it was only then that you discovered how good or poor the snaps were. Good or bad, out of focus, tops of heads missing - you paid for the lot. Family cameras were purchased and then kept for many years - hard to imagine in these days when everyone wants the latest model and cameras, and phones are changed every couple of years.

Earliest picture of me posing with my sister,

In the earliest photo of me as a baby, I appear to be wearing a baby's dress which I suspect had been my sisters. My pram looked as if it was designed to participate in the D Day landings and again had probably served for my sister and brother. I have very few memories of my earliest years. I do recall one time when my Dad was dressing me and he was bent over with one of the hand rolled cigarettes he was fond of hanging out of his mouth. I was wreathed in smoke, and I can still remember the sweet smell of the tobacco. Another time I was lying in my parents' bed, and I was fascinated by the sparkles in the dark wooden wardrobe as the sun shone on it. It looked like it was set with tiny diamonds. I discovered later that it was in fact powdered glass which had impregnated the wood after a bomb blew out the windows in my parents' first house.

Chapter Two Our house

"Our house in the middle of the street"

My sister and I outside our house in Wordsworth Street

Our street was typical of the many rows of terraced houses that huddled round the docks in Bootle. The houses were owned by a landlord who we did not see or know but we were very familiar with his agent the rent man. He called every week to receive the rent in cash after which he made an entry in the rent book kept by the occupier. He knew the residents well and every trick in the book if a resident tried to evade paying when money was short. The landlord retained a small team of workmen who carried out maintenance on the houses as he was responsible for essential repairs and upkeep of the properties. In reality the houses, built in Victorian times, were poorly constructed compared to modern dwellings. They were not insulated and were very draughty and damp. My brother always claimed to have learnt to swim in his small back bedroom. The workmen were located in a small builder's yard at the back of our house, and we were often first in the queue to have work done as my Mum (or Mam as I called her when young) would be round to the yard in short order if we were made to wait. She often would provide the workmen with cups of tea and biscuits to keep them sweet. The house had a tiny front garden with a small wooden fence and the ubiquitous privet hedge. We kids used the leaves of the privet to fashion our home-made kazoos. We folded a leaf, carefully pinched a piece out with our thumb nail, placed it between our thumbs and blew. It made a glorious racket particularly when several of us blew it in chorus. A step led up to the front door and housewives were fanatical about keeping those steps clean. You could always see them knelt down with a bucket, scrubbing brush and bottle of "Aunt Sally" soap and then applying a final finish of a line drawn with a donkey stone across the front of the step. There was a small vestibule behind the front door and a vestibule door. This was very useful as the front door was never closed during the day and the vestibule door kept out the wind and weather. It did not have a lock and in truth there were few concerns about security. There was little of value in our homes and people were always about in the street and so not much opportunity for would be thieves to go unnoticed. Even in the evenings and night when front doors were closed many people kept a front door key on a string that could be retrieved through the letter box. A small narrow hallway led to the stairs and the doors to the parlour and kitchen. Fitted carpets were an unknown luxury to us in those days. Most rooms in the house had linoleum floor coverings. The kitchen and parlour had a large square of carpet which covered the central part of the room, but the bedrooms only had small rugs beside the beds. The parlour was used rarely and contained our best furniture. It was a room for receiving guests and for special occasions. In the event of a death, it was where the deceased would be placed before the funeral so that family and neighbours could come and pay their respects. The night before the funeral would often involve drinking, saying the Rosary with the local priest and people gathering to remember the life of the deceased and this was very reminiscent of the Irish tradition of the

"Wake". As a child I can remember glimpsing images from the street of people laid out in their coffins with candles burning beside them. When the funeral cortege set out all the curtains in the street would be drawn and the residents would line the street to show their respect. Our parlour had the luxury of a three-bar electric fire with a fake coal fire effect produced by an orange bulb under a plastic transparent bed of coal. It even produced a realistic flittering effect courtesy of a small revolving bladed rotor above the bulb. The room housed a small gas meter and electric meter, and we were always filling it with shilling coins but even so there would be a mad dash to find a coin when the lights went out while we were listening to the wireless or when the gas ran out while the tea was being cooked. We always looked forward to the regular visits of the man who came to empty the meter as for some reason we always got a pile of coins returned. In December the Christmas tree was located in the window and the curtains were never drawn at that time. Every house did the same and it produced a warm seasonal glow in the street on those dark winter nights. This was the only exterior illumination in those days in stark contrast to the light shows on offer on most houses these days. The kitchen was actually a small family cum dining room. There was a small wooden table with four chairs, a small two-seater sofa and two small armchairs. This was where the family spent most of the time. A wireless provided entertainment and the family could catch up on each other's daily news. A coal fire provided warmth and apart from the electric fire in the parlour, was the only form of heating in the house. There were fire grates in two of the bedrooms, but they were never lit. Lighting the fire was a chore and a skill to which I was initiated when deemed old enough. It began by preparing strips of wood which had to be split with a small hand axe in the backyard. This was a very satisfying task. These were laid in crisscross fashion across balls of newspaper laid in the grate. After that coals from a coal scuttle kept in the kitchen were placed carefully across the wood. A match was applied and then hopefully the coal would eventually begin to burn. To give the process a boost a small shovel could be placed across the opening of the fire and then a large sheet of newspaper placed across this. This created a greater draught to "draw" the flames, but you had to be watchful and get the timing right as, if left too long, the newspaper would suddenly darken and burst into flames. This happened often and entailed frantic attempts to force the flaming paper into the grate. There was something hugely satisfying in creating a roaring fire which probably harks back to our time spent in the caves attempting to protect ourselves from sabre toothed tigers. It is interesting to see the present popularity of log burning fires in modern homes but easy to understand. Nothing is cosier or more comforting than sitting round a flickering coal fire with the family on a cold, dark winter evening. I can easily recall the sounds of the hissing coal, the warmth, the smell and the pictures you could see in the flames. You don't get that with central heating! Having a coal fire meant an occasional visit from the chimney sweep. This was a complicated and messy business which entailed soot-coloured sheets placed around the fire grate to protect the room, in theory, and then the sweep would push his brushes, which had to be screwed together, up the flue bringing down bucket loads of filthy soot. We children, fascinated by the whole process, would rush out into the street to see the very interesting view of the brush emerging triumphantly from the chimney pot. Of course by the end of this, despite the dust sheets, the whole kitchen would be covered in a fine layer of black soot which would take hours of furious cleaning to remove but having the chimney swept was a necessary chore as those who neglected to have this done were in danger of the dreaded chimney fire when the accumulated soot in the flue would burst into flames and send sheets of flames shooting spectacularly into the air from the chimney pot. Having the chimney swept was not cheap and my Dad, always confident that he could make as good a job of something as any tradesman, decided to do it himself. He borrowed a set of brushes and set about the task despite my Mum's sensible reservations. All went well until after the brush smoothly exited the chimney pot and my Dad found it was stuck and despite his best efforts, he failed to extract it. For many days we were left chilled to the bone as we could not light the fire and we had the dubious honour of living in the only house in the street sporting a brush sticking out of our chimney pot. Eventually, after swallowing his pride, Dad had to call in the chimney sweep to retrieve the brush. A fact of life at that time was because everyone had a coal fire, when it was foggy, the smoke would combine with the fog to produce the infamous "smog". At times this could be really dense, and I can remember times when you literally would be unable to see your outstretched hand in front of your face. The smog not only greatly reduced visibility it also had the effect of deadening sound, and it was eerie walking through the streets as ghostly figures loomed out of the gloom and drifted silently past before quickly disappearing again. Games of hide and seek and kick the can became surreal and were lifted into another dimension and we had tremendous fun, hardly noticing the acrid smell of the smog and absolutely not registering the damage it was almost certainly inflicting on our respiratory systems.

A door from the kitchen led through to what we called the back kitchen. This was in fact the room we would now call the kitchen although it more resembled a scullery. It had a copper boiler for supplying hot water, a few cupboards and worktop space, a small gas stove and a Belfast sink with a wooden draining board and a single cold-water tap. This was the only source of water in the house. The tap often dripped and my Dad always seemed to be replacing the washer which was an essential DIY skill at that time. There was no 'fridge of course. Food was kept in a food safe, and milk and butter kept in water to keep cool. The need to store and refrigerate large amounts of food was not necessary as the weekly or even monthly shop of modern times was non-existent. Shopping for meals was a daily event for most and food was purchased fresh from the wide variety of local shops. The room had a small window over the sink with a panoramic view of the facing back yard wall just a few feet away. A door led to the back yard. This was fairly narrow and had a clay tile floor. It was surrounded by a whitewashed brick wall on all sides which separated us from our neighbours and the backyard entry which we kids called the "jigger". My Dad had built a wooden shed which filled the space between the back kitchen and the outside toilet, although there was a small gap which housed the coal store. The shed provided shelter for my Dad's motor bike and was also used as a small workshop. He fancied himself as a DIYer, although that phrase was not in use then and he would turn his hand to anything. It contained his large collection of tools and was a fascinating place to poke around in when I could sneak in because it was usually out of bounds. Dad loved pottering about in the shed and could turn his hand to many tasks and repairs. For example, he had an antique metal shoe last with which he carried out all shoe repairs for the family. I can picture him now bent over the last with pins stored between his lips and a small hammer in his hand as he fixed new soles on a pair of shoes. His shed was an Aladdin's cave of various items of equipment, nails, screws, nuts and bolts and many other bits and pieces. When out and about he never failed to stop and pick up a screw or a nut lying on the road which would be placed in a jar and added to his collection. If something needed repairing Dad would disappear to his shed and after much searching and banging, he would emerge triumphantly with just the right screw or nut needed to effect the repair. He made all sorts of things in the shed. One time he built a superb model sailing boat for my brother which he sailed on the boating lake in the park in Crosby. Another time he made me a wooden puppet with which I intended to practise to become a puppeteer. Unfortunately, as he was completing it, I contracted measles and was quite poorly. He gave me the finished puppet to cheer me up, but I was too unwell to bother with it. The strange thing is that if I see a wooden puppet now (they sell them in craft shops and The Works) I feel unwell and distinctly uncomfortable. Our tin bath was stored in the shed. Bath night was usually Sunday night, and this was a time consuming and complicated process. The bath was brought into the kitchen and filled with hot water from the copper boiler. Then it was family bathing in strict order with adults first then the children by age and as I was the youngest, I was last in. The expression "throwing the baby out with the bath water," originated with this practice as by that time the water would be so cloudy that the baby could not be seen. The process ended with Dad tipping the water down the backyard. Years later my wife and I visited "Susannah Place" in the Rocks in Sydney Australia. A set of four terraced two up two down houses, they tell the story of early settlers, and the houses are maintained to represent different time periods. There is a guided tour, and we were with a group of Australian visitors. The final house reflects life in the 1950's and as we stood in the kitchen an Australian asked a question. He said, "I've seen the outside dunnie (toilet) but where is the bathroom?" The guide pointed to a tin bath in the backyard and explained the process of family bath night. "You can't imagine what it must have been like for the youngest child to bathe in that cold, dirty water," she said as the Australians shuddered in disgust, but I was nodding my head and thinking to myself "Yep, I sure can!" Our outside toilet was functional and not a place to linger. It had a wooden stable door, an old metal cistern placed high on brackets with a long chain fitted with a wooden handle and a large wooden plank of a toilet seat with a round hole in it. My Mum seemed to be always cleaning the toilet bowl with bleach and scrubbing the wooden toilet seat. The walls were whitewashed and a hanger on the door held strips of toilet paper or at times, newspaper. A paraffin tilley lamp hung from a hook near the cistern to provide light and a little heat to, hopefully, stop the pipes and toilet bowl water freezing up in the winter, although I can recall everything freezing solid during the bleak winter of '62-'63. This necessitated Dad pouring kettles of boiling water down the pan while we kids waited with legs crossed hoping for a thaw! In later years Dad ran a wire from the house into the toilet and fitted an electric light. We thought this was wonderful and made trips to the toilet just before bed on dark winter nights, often wearing our wellies, far less daunting. On one famous occasion my brother went to the toilet and to his great surprise discovered a gypsy flower seller sitting on the loo! He quickly closed the door and returned to the house as she unhurriedly finished her ablutions exited calmly through the back yard door and returned to her attempts to sell flowers door to door in the street.

Mum's state of the art, high tech, washing machine

Also in the backyard were a galvanised zinc dolly tub, dolly stick and plunger which were used for all the family's washing before the purchase of a small top loading washing machine years later. Usually on Mondays, water would be heated up in the copper boiler, a process which filled the back kitchen and indeed the whole house, with steam. Soiled washing would be placed in the dolly tub, which had been filled with scalding water and soap flakes and then Mum would furiously attack this with the dolly stick which looked like a milking stool attached to a pole. This was hard work and would be followed by the plunger to further agitate the washing. Washing was removed and the soiled water replaced with fresh hot water to rinse everything. The clothes and bedding were then run through a metal mangle with large wooden rollers to remove most of the water and then everything was hoisted up on a washing line which ran the length of the yard. Fingers were then crossed, and an anxious eye applied to the sky to watch for rain. Pristine washing on the line was a source of pride for housewives as they knew their neighbours would run an appraising eye over their efforts. I often suppress a smile now when my wife says she has "done the washing", a process the physical demands of which requires only the opening and closing of a door. The only thing that has not really changed I suppose is ironing although in the 1950's this usually involved a flat iron which constantly needed heating on a stove.

Upstairs the house had a small landing with doors leading to three bedrooms - no bathroom of course. There was a loft accessed by a small hatch on the landing but because the roof was slate and pointed with mortar which crumbled and fell over time the loft was so dusty that nothing could be stored there. All the windows in the house were sash. They were difficult to open and because the sashes were complicated to repair many were faulty and some had to be propped up with a piece of wood or a book when opened. As the house was not insulated and there was no central heating it was extremely cold upstairs in the winter. Beds were dressed with sheets, blankets, and a candlewick bedspread but when extremely cold this was supplemented with overcoats. It was not uncommon to dress under the covers to avoid braving the cold in pyjamas and there would sometimes be ice on the inside of the windows. In this event a penny could be warmed by breathing on it and this was used to make two peepholes to gaze out and asses the weather. Even so a trip down the yard in the freezing cold still waited for you before breakfast. Like many at the time our family believed in the great benefits of porridge for breakfast which not only filled you up but also provided inner warmth to ward off the cold – it stuck to your ribs as my Dad used to say. Then off to school, or at weekends and holidays out to play in the street whatever the weather. Whether in school uniform or not, in winter I was always protected from the elements by my liberty bodice. This seems rather odd looking back because it was actually a piece of clothing designed for women and girls but all the boys I knew wore them in winter. Its warm, fleecy fabric was very efficient in keeping out the cold and mine, like many others, had a medal of Our Lady pinned to it to keep me safe just in case.

Chapter Three Our street

"Street life, what a life"

Our street lay between Marsh Lane and Peel Road. Most of the houses were identical to ours except for the prefabs and the houses bordering the main roads which were bigger. We were very envious of the people who lived in the prefabs. They were bright, modern with a form of central heating, hot and cold running water, and a modern bathroom with an inside toilet. They even had a garden instead of a backyard with a picket fence instead of a wall. Our street was designated a play street. It had a sign at both entrances with black letters on a white background which prohibited all vehicles between 8am and sunset unless calling at premises in the street. This made it a fairly safe environment for children and to my recollection only one resident had a car. My Dad had a motor bike and later a sidecar and one or two others had a motorbike or scooter but most if they had any vehicle at all had a bike. Even on the main roads traffic was very light compared to modern times. We played in the street and the surrounding areas all day. Children had a lot more freedom in those days and mostly it was generally considered to be safe. We were rarely on our own and most times in a large group of mixed ages. The street provided a lot of entertainment. The middle part of the street adjacent to the prefabs had an area of smooth concrete road surface rather than the tar macadam which covered the rest of the road. I suspect this was part of the repair works after the houses there were bombed and destroyed. We called this the "Smoothie" and it was a brilliant place to roller skate, often with one skate because the other would be borrowed by a friend who had no skates of their own. Forget the idea of modern roller boots. Our skates had metal wheels, were constructed with a metal frame and had leather straps and buckles to attach them to your shoes. I became quite good on the skates. Years later on a cruise with my wife I decided to try the ship's roller rink, much against her strong advice. She envisaged me being carried off the ship on a stretcher. To her surprise and somewhat of my own I have to say, after a shaky start I was soon zooming round the rink leaving many of the younger people in my wake. All that time spent on the Smoothie over fifty years before paid off. The Smoothie was also a great surface to race our carts. These were vehicles constructed from planks, packing cases and old pram wheels. They were steered with the feet or by a length of clothesline attached to the front axle. Usually built for two, you took turns pushing or steering. A well-built cart was a prized possession. The street had other features which we made use of. Just outside our house at our end of the street there was a gas streetlamp. This had a clockwork timer but originally was lit and extinguished daily by a gas lighter with the aid of a small ladder leant against a horizontal bar below the glass light surround. The lamp was our equivalent of a multi-gym and was used for a wide variety of activities. In the winter it was a goal post for our football matches, the other post being a coat or bag on the other side of the street. These matches could last all day with fluid teams which would change as players were called in to dinner, as we called lunch, or tea as we called dinner! The end of the game was only called when darkness descended. We played with a plastic football and probably the best of these was the "Wembley Trophy" which was of very high quality. Not everyone owned a football and if you did you usually called the shots on team selection and often on the interpretation of the laws of the game! We would try our best not to upset the ball owner as this might result in him or her taking their ball home. In summer the lamppost served as our cricket stumps and the lamppost had a very convenient band around it just at the height the bails would be. The bar on the lamppost was useful as a horizontal beam to perform acrobatics on or to fix a swing to. The girls in the street would attach one end of their skipping rope to the lamppost and often this rope would stretch right across the street and accommodate an impressive number of participants as they skipped and sang songs like "On a mountain stands a lady", "The farmer's in his den" and "I had the scarlet fever". On dark nights the warm glow from the lamp provided a convenient place simply to hang about and chat. All in all, that lamppost was a very valuable and welcome resource which we kids took full advantage of.

Another source of entertainment was the back entries and their back yard walls. Our chase games sometimes involved running along the walls and an initiation rite for our street gang was to jump from the wall on one side of the entry to the wall on the other side. This took strength, skill and not a little courage but was a source of great pride and achievement if successful. Not everyone was first time, and some sustained fairly painful injuries in the attempt which then had to be explained to parents. The "jiggers" were also the place where we undertook our version of big game hunting. This entailed going equipped with some match boxes and a thick elastic band cut to make a long length. Part of the elastic was wound round the hand with a long length left dangling. All set we would quietly make our way into the jigger in search of the huge blue bottle and green bottle flies which were always present in the warmer months as this was where the rubbish bins were located. It required patience, stealth, and skill to creep up on a resting fly, take careful aim by pulling back the loose end of the elastic and then, hopefully splattering the fly. After the hunt the winner would be the hunter with the most flies in their match boxes. Looking back this seems a revolting activity and probably was, but at the time we thought it was great fun!

Towards one end of our street there was a small yard and buildings which in the past we were told had been a small diary. In our time we called it the "Bleachie" as it was used to store and distribute bleach. The place would be deserted at night and then we could climb over the wall and use one of the large metal storage tanks, which for some reason had been turned on its side, as our gang's den. We would plan many activities and escapades in our den and although we used it for years, we were never discovered or prevented from using it as our base. This was probably because we had the good sense to realise that if we did not damage or disturb anything then we had a good chance of being left alone.

Past the "Bleachie" and through the jigger was the "Debbo", coined from the word debris. This was an open space at the end of a terrace row bordering the backyards of the properties on Peel Road. It was the result of the demolition of a heavily bombed house. It was actually on Bibby's Lane, but we claimed it as our own and it became of huge importance as Bonfire Night approached because this was where we had our bonfire. This seems amazing to me now as it was not a huge space; it was directly adjacent to the side of a house and very close to the backyards and sheds of the houses and shops on Peel Road. I can only imagine the heat that must have radiated through the wall of the adjacent house as the fire roared and the anxiety of the residents on Peel Road as drifting embers settled in their yards and sheds. In fact, one year the storage shed in the back yard of our local chippy was set on fire, something that even the

Luftwaffe had failed to achieve in the Blitz. Thankfully this was quenched by the combined efforts of the chippy owners who lived over the premises and we local children who wanted to protect our beloved local treasure. It strikes me as very odd that this practice was tolerated by the adult population of the area or indeed by the local authorities but despite the dangers, I cannot recall anyone suggesting that the Bonfire was a bad idea and the whole thing only came to a halt when the local council built a new electric substation on the "Debbo" to cope with the increasing demand for electricity. But for many years it had remained the place where we maintained the great British tradition of Bonfire Night. We were very proud of our Bonfire, and it took the collective efforts of all the young people in the street to ensure its success. It was a masterpiece of organisational and logistical planning. The older teenagers took the lead with us younger kids as the willing foot soldiers. Work began weeks before as materials began to be collected for the fire. We roamed far and wide to collect wood and anything that would burn. The docks area was a fruitful place to forage and in those more relaxed times it was easier to gain access to the docks. Brocken packing cases and pallets were always to be found and no one seemed to mind us taking them. It was also a good time for people to clear out and get rid of items from their houses and yards. These materials were often left in the back entries waiting for us to collect them. Wood and other materials were then stored on the "Debbo" and as the 5th of November approached this was constructed into an ever-growing cone shaped heap. I would like to say that everything collected was freely donated or foraged legitimately but you sometimes spotted perfectly good sections of garden fences and even toilet seats amongst the steadily growing pile! The problem was that this collection now had to be guarded against the devious envy of rival gangs who saw an easier way to build their own bonfire. Guards were posted and as the big night approached the older teenagers would take turns to remain on guard all through the night. If all went well the final job was to light the fire. The timing of this was vital. Too early and it was all over too quickly. Too late and the younger children might miss the best part of the fire. Lighting the fire could be difficult and dangerous. If there had been wet weather some combustible fuel would be flung on the wood to help the fire take. Often there would be an almighty "woosh" as the fuel ignited but singed eyebrows and eyelashes were a small price to pay for getting things off to a good start. Bonfire nights were always freezing unlike in these days of mixed-up seasons. It was wonderful to feel the heat from the fire and see the flames dancing into the air, knowing that all the hard work and planning had paid off. Sometimes we stayed too close to the fire, and I remember my Mum remonstrating with me one year when I returned home with my wellies partly melted.

The tradition of burning the Guy was followed which now strikes me as strange as we were nearly all Catholics and here we were commemorating the failure of a Catholic conspirator in a plot to replace a Protestant King with a Catholic monarch. We made Guys weeks before the 5th of November to collect money and one year I had an idea to make it easier. We simply "chose" a volunteer, one of the twins in our street gang, dressed him in his duffel coat which we stuffed with newspaper to make him look more genuine and then with mask and gloves fitted we were all set. He would be laid in a cart and from then on all he had to do was keep still. We would wheel him round the streets collecting pennies for the Guy. A good place to locate was outside the local pubs of which there were many. As the drinkers left, feeling more generous after copious amounts of beer, they usually were very receptive to our requests of "A penny for the Guy mister". They often would comment on how realistic our Guy was. Money was shared out amongst the gang, and this was used to purchase fireworks. In truth we were not interested in pretty, colourful fireworks. We were only interested in rockets, ripraps, and most of all bangers. Bangers cost a penny, but we favoured two penny "Dreadfuls" which created a huge bang. We kept the bangers in a bundle secured by an elastic band and shoved in a pocket and they were a source of great amusement. I would be horrified if my children had got up to the same tricks we did. A game of chicken would be to stand in a circle and all light a banger held in a stretched-out hand. As the banger fuse fizzed away, we would wait for somebody's nerve to desert them. Once they dropped the banger, we all could. On more than one occasion I witnessed bangers exploding in somebody's hand thankfully with no serious injury. The creditability of this dangerous game was undermined when one bright spark discovered that by carefully cutting off the end of the banger the gunpowder could be removed which made it a risk-free challenge for them. Another trick was to carefully float a lit banger in the pool of water which collected near a drain which was invariably blocked at one end of the street. The firework propelled by its fizzing fuse would shoot across the water before exploding and creating a spray of water which, with any luck, would soak unwary onlookers. At other times the dirty pool of water was often deep and wide enough to sail small wooden boats on. I cannot ever remember that drain being unblocked by the council.

On Bonfire Night some adults would attend the fire with younger children and sparklers and more gentle fireworks would be in evidence. Later as the flames died down our street gang would be left to our own devices and bangers, ripraps and rockets would be going off constantly. Later still we would settle down and place potatoes in the hot ashes. I still think that nothing could ever match the taste of those baked spuds, tossed from hand to hand as they were cooling and then savoured on a freezing night huddled round the glowing embers. We went home eventually, stinking of smoke, our wellies partly melted but with full stomachs and happy that our Bonfire Night had been a huge success. Roll on Christmas!

Chapter Four Annual street activities

Springtime was marked by the May procession. We would dress up in various outfits, often adult clothes adapted for the occasion, with the girls in the prettiest dresses they could manage. Possession of a bridesmaid's dress would often be a major factor in one of the girls being chosen as our May Queen and she would be decked with flowers gathered in various ways, often obtained surreptitiously from nearby gardens. We would then parade around the street and visit local shops and pubs on Peel Road and Marsh Lane to collect donations, often competing with processions from other streets but because this was a very old tradition, which adults had participated in, in their day, they were often very generous. We always eagerly anticipated the Bootle Carnival and Litherland Gala in May. They were highlights of the social year and featured the crowning of the May Queen. Both began with very elaborate processions with lavishly decorated floats, Morris dancers, pipe bands, brass bands, and lots of participants in fancy dress. A lot of local businesses sponsored a float and I particularly remember the "Full Swing" float, a popular brand of lemonade which always featured a young girl on a real swing decorated with flowers. Many girls envied her and wished they could take her place. There were often several bands from local scout groups, the Boys' Brigade, and local branches of the Orange Lodge. You could hear the booming of the big drums and the skirl of the bagpipes from some distance, and it was always a very stirring sound. Pride of place in the procession was always reserved for the May Queen sitting resplendent in a black limousine wearing a beautiful ball gown. Crowds would line the streets to watch the procession and we always ensured we were in place early to get the best view. The Bootle procession ended in the North Park while Litherland's terminated in the Bryant and May sports field in Litherland. The crowning of the May Queen followed and lots of activities like Morris dancing, police dog demonstrations and various games. There were stalls for food and drink and

Wallis's Fair would always do a roaring trade. We particularly enjoyed rides on the "Speedway" and the "Waltzer". The "Speedway" operator always used to shout over the tannoy "Do you want to go faster?" as the girls used to scream and the boys did their best to look cool. We always admired the young men of the Fair on the "Waltzer" who used to stand on the ride and slap the carriages to make them spin faster. In the evenings as the light began to fade the whole place seemed magical to us with the coloured lights and the pop music blaring over the tannoys. With any luck we would have a few pennies left to buy a candy floss to eat on the walk home. The long days of summer were spent in various ways, and we would often venture farther afield, but more on that later. In the street, at weekends and in holidays, straight after breakfast we would be out and about until late at night, calling in at home for brief pit stops for dinner and tea. Games included football, cricket, skating on the Smoothie, carting and several chase and hide and seek games. The most popular of the latter were "Lally O" and "Kick the Can". They were very similar. One person would be "on", hide their eyes and count to a hundred, which was challenging for some. The rest would scatter and hide and there were many places to choose - front gardens, backyards, jiggers, and jigger walls. A child hiding, if spotted by name by the person who was "on" had to return to the "Den", usually located by the lamppost. If all the children were caught in this way the game was over, but an "unspotted" person could free everyone in the Den by racing past shouting "Lally o co co" or kicking the can placed by the Den. Often there were disputes of course and this would result in the call of "All in" when everyone gathered to discuss and hopefully resolve the issue.

Another popular game in summer was a version of marbles which we called "ollies" or "onks". This was played in the gutter alongside the kerbs on either side of the street. Rules were fluid but essentially two players took turns to flick an ollie with their thumbs to try and hit their opponent's ollie. If successful they kept the marble and the better players often built up huge collections. "Steelies", metal ball bearings, were particularly highly prized and it was a major disappointment to lose one.

Playing war was a very popular activity. As many parents had served in the forces and Army Stores were still full of World War 2 ex-military supplies, we participated in our war games extremely well equipped. Tin helmets, even the German variety, gas masks, binoculars, weapons such as rifles and handguns (made safe hopefully) and a wide variety of military clothing gave our games an authenticity which would be impossible to match now. Usually, you had to take your turn as a German, but we recognised that without an enemy the games were useless. The British always won of course and if you were playing the part of the enemy an impressive show of being shot would always win you the admiration of the other players. A variation of this game was "Cowboy and Indians". I am not sure if my grandchildren or even my children have ever seen a "Western" but they were a staple diet on the TV and cinema when I was young. Again, we would dress up and most kids had a cowboy outfit, and some had what we would now call Native American costumes. Such was our naivety in those pre-politically correct times that we all accepted that the cowboys always won, and the Indians were the bad guys. A good way to impress in these games was to replicate the Pidgin English which we all knew was how the Indians spoke. How happy we were in our ignorance and the casual racist and historically inaccurate diet we were fed in those days by Hollywood and the TV programme makers. On other occasions our war games consisted of two sides fighting it out armed with elastic bands strung together. One end was placed around the thumb and the other end around the first finger to form a type of catapult. This was your weapon and bullets were made of paper or card folded into a "V" shape. These were fired at the enemy and could create quite a sting if hitting exposed flesh. Of course, this was highly dangerous and made more so by the idiots who substituted metal staples for cardboard pellets. It was only pure luck that no one was blinded.

The second week in June was always an interesting time. Although most people in my street were Catholics there were some Protestants and Bootle Village across Stanley Road was regarded as a strong area of support for the Orange Lodge. It is a curious fact that Bootle and Liverpool still retained some of the prejudices that earlier generations had carried from Ireland when they migrated. Sectarian violence, often centred around St. Patrick's Day and the 12th. of July, could be traced back to the middle of the 19th. Century and continued until well into the 20th. Century. Thousands turned out for the marches on the "Twelfth" and given that Liverpool, by the end of the 19th. Century was the largest Roman Catholic diocese in England, the potential for trouble was palpable. After the Second World War religion and sectarianism was in decline but problems remained into the 1960s and beyond. In his three-part television series on the city in 2008 Alexei Sayle joked that Liverpool was the only place in England when if you were asked if you were Orange the question was not about your mobile phone network. Bootle still has 20 lodges and on the 12th. of July they meet with members of other lodges to march through the streets of Southport. In the 1960s the Bootle lodges after disembarking from the Southport train would march down Marsh Lane but instead of making their way directly back in the direction of Bootle Village they would instead parade in the direction of the docks. This would take them into the predominantly Catholic area and past several pubs. There would be a large audience keen to hurl insults at the marches and we children would participate enthusiastically. With any luck, as many on both sides were liberally fuelled with drink, scuffles would break out watched with great interest by us younger members of the crowd. Secular schools reinforced much of this prejudice and growing up I hardly knew any non-Catholics. Merseyside still has the highest proportion of faith schools to population in the country. There were some mixed marriages, but they tended to be the exception and were certainly frowned on by the Catholic priests. A few years later, after we had moved to Netherton, my sister met a boy who lived just around the corner and after visiting his house told us that his family had a large picture of a man on a horse in their living room. "That's King Billy," my Dad said with concern in his voice. As it happened my Dad and my sister's boyfriend, Kenny, got on famously and they were kindred spirits in many ways. When they were engaged and due to be married, though, we learned that this was not well received by Kenny's Dad's lodge, and he was asked to leave the lodge band which was regarded as a valued position even though he could not actually play the squeeze box he carried on parades! My sister planned to marry in our local church, and this involved meeting with the parish priest. But Catholic clergy by this time had a pragmatic approach and as long as the couple planned to bring up any children in the faith and the non-Catholic partner took some instruction (although there was no requirement to convert) then they were content. Kenny had to attend a number of evening sessions of instruction with the parish priest, but these proved not to be onerous after the priest discovered that they both shared an interest in horse racing. The majority of the time intended for religious instruction, in fact, was spent pouring through "The Racing Post" to pick runners and riders for forthcoming meetings.

After the summer it was conker season. To collect conkers, we had to travel to find horse chestnut trees as green and tree filled areas were in short supply in our immediate neighbourhood. The best conkers were those kept for a year to harden. Soaking them in vinegar helped in this process, some even baked them briefly in the oven but coating them in nail varnish was regarded as cheating. A hole carefully drilled in the conker was then threaded, usually with an old shoelace and then you were all set. A conker not used in competition was a "oner". An opponent had to be chosen carefully and then turns were taken to hit the other conker. If the strings became entangled the first player to shout "strings" had an extra turn. The end of the game was when one conker split and fell off the string. A "oner" then became a "twoer" or even a "threeer" or "fourer" or more as the winning conker assimilated the previous score of the losing conker. There were legendary tales and boasts of mighty "twentiers" or "fortiers" but I never possessed one. A few years ago, I despaired to read of schools that were planning to ban conkers on the grounds of health and safety. Why? How ridiculous to consider ending the ancient and noble art of conker playing.

As the end of October loomed our thoughts turned to "Knick Knock Night" and "Duck Apple Night". The American tradition of Halloween had not yet arrived on these shores and "Knick Knock Night", observed on the 30th of October, was simply when we knocked on doors and ran away. Over the years on Merseyside this has morphed into "Missie" night, short for "Mischief Night" and it has become a licence for vandalism and criminal damage making it an anxious night for many residents. The police are out in force but even so there are many reports of bricks smashing windows, eggs being thrown at houses and cars being damaged. In our day the evening was considered a minor nuisance and largely tolerated by adults. We did, however, try to be inventive. One of our more successful tricks was to tie fishing line, virtually invisible in the dark, around the door knocker of a house and then carefully tie the other end around the knocker of the facing house across the street. A tug on the line and then we would retreat to a safe hiding place. A resident would open the door to see who was knocking, find no one there and close the door. This would activate the knocker on the facing house across the street and the process would be repeated. With any luck this could go on for several minutes or until our stifled laughter gave the game away. I would imagine many residents on Merseyside would welcome a return to those more innocent and simpler ways of observing this particular night. The following evening had no sign of vampire costumes or trick or treating. Instead, Dads would fill the galvanised bathtub which then had nuts thrown in and apples floated in it. Children would be blindfolded and kneeling down would try to bite an apple or even duck their heads to try to retrieve a nut from the bottom of the tub. Of course, everyone became soaked amid much laughter and fooling about. Sometimes apples would be strung from the pulley clothes drier, which was attached to the ceiling over the fire in the kitchen, as an additional challenge. Usually, the evening ended with Dad roasting chestnuts on the coal shovel over the fire as we sat close to the flames to dry off. I can still recall the wonderful smell of those chestnuts and of course the delicious taste. Then off to bed knowing that the next day we would return to our preparations for Bonfire Night.

After Bonfire Night there was a brief interlude but very soon our thoughts would turn to Christmas. Unlike today when you hear Christmas songs in shops in October and decorations and lights begin to appear in November, not much happened until well into December. Schools did begin rehearsals for Christmas earlier than this, but many households would not decorate their homes until as late as the third week of December or even later. Exterior lighting for houses was non-existent but Christmas Trees in parlour windows did provide some Christmassy glow in the street. Many had real trees, but we were very modern and had an artificial tree! In truth it was a very poor relation in comparison with modern trees. It was about four or five feet high with branches that most closely resembled bottle brushes. This was strung with an ancient set of multi coloured lights with large bulbs which were always blowing causing all the lights to go off. Of course, you could not know which one had failed so this involved a complicated and lengthy process of unscrewing bulbs in sequence and inserting a new one until the lights finally came back on. This was Dad's unenviable task accompanied always by dark murmurings and whispered curses until finally a cry of triumph signalled success. Sometimes in frustration he would resort to stripping the bulbs off the tree and vigorously shaking them which, surprisingly, often worked. The tree was further decorated with some purchased baubles and tinsel but also homemade paper chains. An angel always had pride of place at the top of the tree, and this was by tradition placed there by the youngest member of the family. By today's standards the tree was very modest, but we were very proud of it. There were no other decorations in the parlour, but we went to town in our family room, the kitchen. We children spent hours making paper chains from coloured sticky paper and draping them from the ceiling and walls until the room looked like a winter wonderland. It was always a depressing time when we took down the decorations on the twelfth night - the room always looked so bleak and drab.

Once the decorations were up, we children could then organise our carol singing activities. We would write out the words to a few carols, rehearse a couple of times and then armed with a couple of candle lanterns we were all set. As soon as it was dark, we would gather and set off. On people's doorsteps we would ensure that the youngest and cutest kids were in the front and then we would knock and belt out our first carol. People were usually very kind and tolerant and would listen to one or two verses before putting a few coins into our proffered tin cans. Sometimes we would be told to get lost as we were the umpteenth set of carollers that evening because we did have many competitors! Despite this we usually made a decent amount which was then shared out equally. Schools had Christmas productions, but they tended to have a religious theme and invariably portrayed the Nativity and did not much resemble the very lavish affairs that schools attempt now. Costumes were always homemade by willing Mums not like the elaborate designs now freely available in supermarkets. I can only remember being in one Nativity when I was cast as a shepherd and dressed in my dressing gown with a tea towel wrapped round my head and secured with a piece of cloth. My elder brother made me practise my lines for weeks so as not to embarrass the family on the night, but he need not have worried. When I entered the stage and approached the stable to visit Baby Jesus, I was word perfect - "Is 'ee within?". My brother was very proud of me! The last day of school before the Christmas holiday was always keenly anticipated as we ended the day with a party. Mums were asked to send in contributions and there was always lots of cake, biscuits and jelly to go round. We would play games like blind man's bluff, musical chairs and statues and we always had a fine time.

Christmas shopping always involved a trip to Liverpool, and this meant a trip on the train from Marsh Lane or the bus. You were spoilt for choice in terms of the bus and there were regular services from the red Ribble buses and green Liverpool Corporation buses along Knowsley Road or Stanley Road into

Town. I always preferred the green Corporation buses with their open back loading access. Young men would show off by jumping on the bus while it was moving or stepping off before the bus came to a complete stop. All the buses had smartly uniformed conductors so there was no waiting when the bus arrived. Everyone boarded quickly and the conductor would collect fares along the way. The buses had leather seats and were kept immaculately clean, often smelling of disinfection in the mornings. Smoking was permitted upstairs and there was often a fog of cigarette smoke hanging in the air causing your clothes to smell of tobacco, but it was worth it for the superior view sitting on the top deck afforded. On the return journey, usually in the dark evening, the bus was lit by very bright round light bulbs which created a warm, cheerful atmosphere in contrast to the gloom outside. In Town my Dad loved to visit "Paddy's Market" on Great Homer Street, nowadays known as "Greatie". It had a large collection of market stalls selling new and second hand goods and always seemed to be crowded but was an excellent place to bag a bargain. There were also a good range of department stores in the city centre - Owen Owen, George Henry Lee, Blackler's, TJ Hughes, Marks and Spencer and Lewis's. Dad's favourite was Lewis's as he always claimed that you could get anything you needed there. It claimed to be the first store in the world to install a Christmas grotto and a visit to see

Father Christmas was always a great treat. It also had wonderful window displays which were always a must to see at Christmas, when Dad did his best to distract us from gazing up at the infamous statue of "Dickie Lewis", the naked statue above the store entrance. Lewis's employed a lot of floor staff, often seemingly standing around doing nothing and this was the origin of the popular Liverpool phrase of "standing round like one of Lewis's". TJ Hughes had a grotto but also featured special shows. One year it was "The Dancing Waters" a spectacular show of coloured water jets and fountains accompanied by classical music. Years later my wife and I visited the "Fountains of Bellagio Show" outside the hotel in Las Vegas and observing the enthusiastic response of the crowded onlookers I couldn't help thinking "So what? TJ Hughes were doing this fifty years ago!" The entertainment also featured the "Pinky and Perky" puppet show which was great fun. This consisted of the two pig puppets dancing about and singing some popular songs which for all the world sounded like the song being played at the wrong speed. Blackler's was sometimes referred to as the Liverpool Macy's because like the famous Manhattan store it was enormous and occupied a whole city block. It also had a grotto, a huge Father Christmas hung in its central stair well and it was renowned for its display of lights decorating the outside of the building. Children could also queue up for a ride on

"Blackie" a rocking horse which is now kept in Liverpool Museum. All in all, Liverpool was a great place for a child to visit at Christmas time.

Christmas Eve was always a magical day as the anticipation for the great day built up. Our house would be filled with the sound of carols and Christmas songs on the wireless and the smells of food being prepared for the following day. One year Dad had this brain wave to buy a turkey chick to raise for Christmas dinner. The chick arrived halfway through the year and was kept in the shed and backyard. It was a friendly bird, was given the name "Cluckie" and inevitably became like a family pet. As December approached Dad grew introspective and his great idea to save money began to look less and less attractive. Just before Christmas he steeled himself to dispatch the bird but just couldn't do it. In the end he sought the assistance of his brother-in-law, who had a more pragmatic disposition, to do the deed. He made sure we children were out of the house, but we were devastated when we discovered that our pet was no more. Needless to say, none of us had much appetite for turkey on Christmas day. In future our birds were purchased ready prepared from the butchers as this had the advantage that we did not know the turkey personally! On Christmas Eve when I was old enough, I joined the family at midnight mass. This was a very atmospheric service with carols and flickering candles creating a warm seasonal glow as you peered at the stable scene with the empty cradle awaiting the birth of the Baby Jesus, although the atmosphere was spoilt on occasions by members of the congregation who had spent the evening in the pub and were clearly the worse for wear. Then a walk home through the quiet streets and bed, hopefully tired enough to sleep and await the visit of Father Christmas. A pillowcase would be placed at the foot of the bed and with any luck, if we had been good and he had read the letter we had sent him, he would fill it with our desired presents. No matter how late we had gone to bed we would always get up early on Christmas morning and reach for the pillowcase at the end of the bed. In those days when budgets were often stretched, we did not have the same lavish expectations that many children have today. Usually, we would have one main present and some less expensive stocking, or in our case pillowcase, fillers. One year I received a small electric train set and in subsequent years might receive an additional engine or piece of rolling stock to add to it. Then there was usually a comic book annual, the "Beano" or "Topper" or in later years a "William" book to add to my collection. Finally, there would usually be a selection box and that would be about it. I was very proud of my train set. It was a Tri-ang set and a rival at that time to Hornby Dublo although in later years the two companies merged. I had a steam engine with rolling stock and later a Canadian Pacific engine and carriages in a blue and yellow livery with working headlights on the engine. I remember the train set had a huge electric transformer which was a solid metal rectangular box which made a loud humming sound when in operation. After we children had opened our presents, we would go downstairs for breakfast and give our parents their presents. These presents never varied - some perfumed toilet water for Mum and half an ounce of Golden Virginia tobacco for Dad - but despite this they always expressed their surprise and delight! Then we would play with our new presents or join our friends in the street to compare our gifts. I can't remember anyone receiving a really expensive gift like a new bicycle, but we were very happy with what we had been given. In fact, as a child the only bikes I had were bikes handed down from my brother and these had been purchased second hand in the first place. Christmas Dinner was eaten about 2 o'clock. It was a rare feast of turkey roast dinner followed by Christmas pudding and mince pies. An additional rarity was that it was accompanied by bottles of beer, brown ale for the adults and shandies for the young people. We felt very grown up and sophisticated, the notion of meals accompanied by wine at that time being beyond our realm of experience. Although we were not particularly fond of the Royalty, Dad was a loyal Labour supporter and a socialist and republican at heart, we always listened respectfully to the

Queen's speech on the wireless wearing our paper crowns but unlike some families at the time we did not go as far as standing for the National Anthem. In the evenings we usually walked to my Dad's sister's house near Bootle Town Hall. His other sister and her family joined us, and we would spend a very pleasant evening playing games and singing songs. It was a large house and always had an enormous Christmas tree in the front room. We would receive further presents and there was always a large spread of food and drinks. Together with our cousins we children were always expected to perform by singing a song or reciting a poem which we would have rehearsed for weeks. I remember one year when my sister and I sang "The Christmas Alphabet". As a reward we were allowed to pick the many chocolate decorations hanging from the tree. Late at night we would walk back home, tired but very content. In the very bad weather of Christmas 1962 I remember my Dad carrying me piggyback as he ploughed through snow which came up to his knees. I had recently read a book about Captain Scott's ill-fated expedition to the South Pole and as I watched my Mum and sister struggle through the snow and gazed out at a Marsh Lane which was unrecognisable and more resembled the frozen wastes of Antarctica, I began to fear a similar fate to that which befell those brave explorers. But I need not have worried as my Dad, as heroic and strong as Captain Oates and his colleagues in my eyes, led us safely home. We may have been freezing and wet, arriving in a cold and unheated house but we were very pleased and happy that once again we had experienced a wonderful Christmas. Looking back those times were magical and the happiest times of my childhood. One year was especially memorable as my Dad took my sister and me to the Empire Theatre Panto. It was in 1959 and a production of "Jack and the Beanstalk" starring Hilda Baker, whose catch phrase was "She knows you know" and Jimmy Clitheroe of the wireless programme "The Clitheroe Kid" a favourite of mine. He was only four foot two inches tall and played the part of a mischievous schoolboy. His catch phrase was "Don't some mothers 'ave em!". Also on the bill were Morecambe and Wise. The latter two were not yet the superstars they would become but they were already quite famous. I remember they came into the audience and stopped by our row to continue their routine. It was great fun. Eric had that gift of provoking laughter with just a look, and they were both masters of the adlib. I watch many so-called modern comedians on TV and despair as they never raise a smile from me with their long rambling anecdotes and stories (there are some notable exceptions). They must watch clips of comic geniuses like Eric and Ernie and Tommy Cooper and weep!

Chapter Five Our Neighbourhood

"In my beautiful neighbourhood"

Our street lay between Marsh Lane and Peel Road and was very close to Knowsley Road and Strand Road. This meant we had easy access to a range of shops, businesses, pubs, and facilities. Mums shopped every day for meals, and they did not have to travel far as grocery stores and a range of butchers and fishmongers were all available. Peel Road had a Costigan's and a Blackledge's which sold pies, meats and the best barm cakes and blackcurrant tarts you could wish for. It also had a Co-op store and you had to remember your Mum's membership number if you were sent to buy something as this was added to your "divi" or dividend which could be used to buy things from the store. Connor's was a newsagents that sold drinks and sweets and a chandlers sold all sorts of household items. We called the chandlers the "Old Man's" as the owner was getting on a bit. He always wore a brown overall and he made the most delicious ice cream which was always a special treat after Sunday roast dinner usually served with slices of banana. Sweets could be purchased in a few shops and for a penny you could buy four fruit salads or black jacks, or you could splash out and buy a sherbet fountain for two pence or maybe four ounces of sherbet lemons for three pence.

Dentists were never short of work in those days and in truth dental hygiene did not feature prominently in our daily routines. I did have a toothbrush, but I cannot remember being encouraged or urged to use it twice a day. Nor did we have regular check-ups or visits to the dentists. A trip to the dentist was only made as a last resort after the sweets had done their damage, toothache had become intolerable and drastic action was required. Dentists were feared and the one we used on Stanley Road was awarded the title "The Butcher" by us kids. Extractions were carried out on a certain day and as you made your way to the surgery you would pass other children holding bloodied cloths to their mouths and being supported by their accompanying parent as they were still feeling woozy after the anaesthetic. As you sat in the waiting room the feeling of dread would intensify and your heart would thud as your name was called and you dragged your feet as you entered the dentist's room. The sight of the ominous looking chair with the large domed light above would make you break into a sweat and as you reluctantly sat it the dentist's nurse would approach. In our case it was his wife, and she would smile and as incongruous as it sounds, she would wave a lollipop in front of your eyes. This was a mere distraction as behind you the dentist would glide forward and quickly slap the rubber mask over your face and despite doing your best to struggle, within seconds everything became dim as you succumbed to the gas. I can still recall the smell of that mask, even now I have an aversion to the aroma of rubber, and I can vividly remember the taste of the horrid gas. After what seemed like an instant the nurse would rudely shake you awake and in pain, swallowing blood and biting down on a large pad of cotton wool, you were escorted out of the room by your parent and supported down a steep flight of stairs, still half unconscious. Visits to the dentist were not for the faint hearted and I still am nervous when I have my regular check-ups. On a trip to Beamish Museum in County Durham recently we visited the dentist's surgery. As I gazed at the chair, manual drill and various devilish instruments a feeling of dread crept over me, and I could not leave the room fast enough. What a different experience it is for my children and grandchildren who are so aware of the importance of dental care and have absolutely no fear of visits to their bright welcoming surgeries and very friendly dentists

Our shoes were normally purchased from a store on Knowsley Road. Shoe shops were very different in those days and consisted of a room surrounded on all sides by stacks and shelves of shoe boxes with several chairs in the middle just like Hobson's shoe shop in the film "Hobson's Choice". The shop assistant used a sliding wooden ladder to reach boxes of shoes that were stacked from floor to ceiling. There was always a wonderful smell of leather permeating the air. The purchase of a new pair of shoes was a special and relatively expensive event and usually a pair which was one or two sizes too large was chosen as they would have to last for quite a time – "allowing room for growth" was the normal rational. I remember my Dad buying me my first pair of football boots. They were proper boots, not like the slippers worn today, which covered the ankles and had a hard toecap. The studs were made of hard rolls of leather and the laces were enormous and had to be wrapped round the heel and under the boot several times. Unlike the rainbow colours popular now all boots in those days were black or brown. Those boots served me for several years and at first had to have newspaper shoved into the toecap to make them fit, but I was very proud of them and always cleaned them and rubbed them with dubbin until they shone. One of our favourite shops was the "Chippy". In those days the food was served in newspaper and a family chippy tea was a real treat to look forward to. You could order a "six" (six pence) of chips and if you were treating a friend the server would actually wrap two separate portions. At the time treating a friend was referred to as "mugging" – "It's ok. I'll mug you". How the meaning of words can change over time. A cheap alternative to chips was a "scallop" which was really shredded potato in batter and bore no relation to the saltwater clam of the same name. There were clothes shops nearby but most shopping for clothing was done on and around Strand Road. This was a bustling area full of independent retailers: green grocers, butchers, fishmongers, boot makers, florists, cycle shops, drapers, tailors, milliners, jewellers, and a whole host of other businesses. When shopping a special treat was to visit Felice's coffee shop on Stanley Road for frothy coffee served in a glass cup. There was a Woolworth's, a British Gas showroom, a wallpaper shop with a machine to cut the protective edges off the paper and even an early form of supermarket called Victor Value on Stanley Road. There were many other shops in the area around Strand Road and Stanley Road and a trip into "town", Liverpool, although always welcome, was never a strict necessity. If money was really tight it was always possible to pick up a bargain in the pawn shop, with its sign of three balls, at the top of our street.

Of more interest to the dads in the street was the large collection of pubs in the local area. On Marsh Lane the Salisbury "Sollie", the Jollys and the Alexandria were popular. There were many other pubs in the local area and in those days most of them had an off licence or "offie". This had a separate door to the street and drink could be purchased to take away. On Sundays some would go with a jug to be filled with beer to be served with lunch and they would carry it carefully back home, the jug covered with a plate.

A popular place for us kids was Peel Road Park which had a collection of swings, slides and other equipment – the "Witches Hat" was always popular. A walk down Knowsley Road took us to North Park. This had a playground, a boating lake for model boats and a paddling pool which was very popular in the summer, although you had to be careful as there always seemed to be broken glass on its concrete floor. This park had the great advantage of having a large area of grass and trees so it was ideal for playing games and of course football and cricket games. It was our chance to wear football boots and play on proper grass. Peel Road had a small snooker hall which was popular with my older brother and his friends. Younger children were not allowed in the hall, but it also had a small non-alcoholic bar which we called the "Drinkie" and they did tolerate us in there. Inside there were a few tables and benches and we felt very grown up sipping our American cream sodas and sarsaparillas. Occasionally the door to the snooker hall would open and we would catch a tantalising glimpse of the tables with the overhead lights and the players bending over to take a shot or standing chalking the end of their cues. It all seemed very mysterious and fascinating to us, and we couldn't wait to be older enough to take part. Across the road on the corner of Tennyson Street stood the local library. I would reach it via the backyard and back entry. I loved it in there and joined at a very early age. It had a children's section and a large collection of fiction and non-fiction books. The librarians were very friendly and helpful often encouraging me to try different books and authors. I found out that you could reserve a book if it was already out on loan and even request a book from another branch. Often, I would spend a good deal of time reading a number of books before choosing the six you were allowed to take home. In particular I enjoyed "William" books "Jennings" and the "Billy Bunter" series as well as adventure books like "Treasure Island" and "Coral Island". The lifestyles of the characters in those books could not have been any more different from mine and I guess that was part of their great attraction. Billy Bunter attended Greyfiars School a fictional public school full of privileged boys from wealthy homes who spent most of their time waiting for a cheque from home – at that time I didn't know what a cheque was. Jennings attended a posh preparatory school while William Brown's family had a cook and housemaid, and his father wore a suit for dinner or tea as we would call it. On the advice of one of the librarians I discovered an interest in science fiction, a staple diet of my reading even now. I would eagerly await the arrival of new batches of books which took place regularly and the librarians would often put aside a book for me that they knew I would like. Many happy hours were spent in that library lost in tales of environments and even worlds, very different to my own. Access to libraries was one of the most valuable and free resources open to us and I remained a member of the local library wherever I lived from that time on.

Although rarely on my own when out and about and despite having some friends in the street who were real hard cases, it was inevitable that if you stood up for yourself you would find yourself in a fight at some point. There were numerous rival groups of kids in the surrounding streets and conflict was always a possibility. My problem was twofold - I would never back down or give in to bullying or intimidation and this usually resulted in me ending up in a fight, often with boys older and bigger than me and, secondly, I was useless at fighting. I was that bad that when shadow boxing my shadow always won! It is a fact that I only ever won one fight and that was against a boy recovering from TB! I hasten to add that I did not provoke the fight and when in full health my opponent would have wiped the floor with me. I am sad to say that his older brother later restored his family's honour with interest. It must have been obvious to my Dad, and a source of some disappointment to him, that I had been runner up in a number of contests because he decided that I needed boxing lessons. My Dad had been something of an amateur boxer and, when in the merchant navy, had championed his ship in matches against opponents from rival ships. Unfortunately, I did not inherit his pugilistic genes and my boxing lessons ended when, demonstrating a right hook, he inadvertently caught me squarely under the chin. I actually flew over the back of the sofa and for the first time in my life saw stars. My Mum, running in from the kitchen, screamed "You've killed him!" while beating my Dad with the tea towel. Luckily there was no serious damage but from that time on I had to fight without the benefit of my Dad's tuition.

Chapter Six Further Afield

"To boldly go where no man has gone before"

Swimming near the sewage outlet in the River Mersey with my sister and cousin

We often ranged further afield, and a popular destination was the beach alongside the River Mersey. At that time Gladstone Dock marked the northern perimeter of the docks complex and after that it was a long beach which stretched up to Southport. It was wonderful to see the golden sands and the twinkling waters of the River Mersey and was a great place to play, explore and spend time. On hot days we would swim in the river and just beyond Gladstone Dock there was a concrete ramp that ran down into the water. This was a very convenient place from which to jump or even dive into the water. Years later I learnt that, in fact, it was the sewage outlet that in those times discharged untreated sewage into the river. We always wondered why huge flocks of seagulls were always so interested in the waters surrounding that concrete ramp. The beach at Seaforth and Crosby was a great place to play cricket and football. Now it is the location of Anthony Gormley's artwork "Another Place", a series of 100 cast iron figures facing the sea. When my brother first saw this, he commented that if some of the figures had been placed closer together, they would have made very convenient goal posts as we had had to make do with folded coats and bags for our games. In a fit of ridiculous hubris Gormley modelled the naked statues on his own body but on seeing them my brother was convinced that he used a large dollop of poetic licence – maybe Gormley did not like the idea of playing second fiddle to Dickie Lewis!

In the summer holidays we would sometimes make the journey to Freshfield for a day on the sand dunes and the beach. This meant a trip on the train. We would go in a large party made up of my gang of friends and my sister's friends who were a couple of years older. Sarah (not her real name) would often join the group. She was a young adult with special needs and had been a member of every generation of street gang for years. Of course, I did not understand this at the time and regarded her simply as a friend and part of the gang. Sarah was extremely sensible and trusted by the adults – she had wheeled many of the babies in the street in their prams for many years, including me. She could be relied upon to look after us on our wider excursions and her physical presence deterred other kids from messing with us but to be honest some of the older boys in our group were tough enough to cope with most situations. Armed with our supplies which usually consisted of jam and lemon curd butties and bottles of water we would make our way up Marsh Lane to the train station. In those days the station was accessed via a covered sloping walkway from the "Lane". The train connected to Liverpool Central and Southport. Although Southport had many attractions you really needed money to make the most of a visit there- the sand dunes cost nothing. We would alight at Freshfield Station and wander past the very large houses on Victoria Road to reach Formby Point. Nowadays there is a protected red squirrel nature reserve located there with restricted access but in our day, you could go where you wished. We would make a base on a large sand dune, and it was possible that we would not see another soul all day. Games of war and hide and seek would follow and we would make ski slopes down the dunes, sliding on our backsides or on pieces of cardboard – we had a fine time. Occasional visits to the sea would follow and depending on the weather, we would paddle or swim. As the evening approached, we would make our way back to the station, tired, hungry, thirsty and sunburned- sun protection was an unknown concept for us at that time. Thirst sometimes prompted us to knock on the door of a big posh house on Freshfield Road to ask if we could have our bottles re-filled with water. Most times the residents were very tolerant and kind to a bunch of scruffy "scallies" from Bootle and on several occasions, biscuits accompanied the water. We would arrive back in Wordsworth Street after a fabulous day which cost us nothing but the train fare although we would have sand in our shoes for the rest of the year.

Another popular activity was a bike ride. Having a bike was a great gift and significantly increased our horizons. Popular destinations included "Froggy Meadow" which lay between Litherland and Crosby and trips along the canal to Netherton. "Froggy Meadow" was an area of wetland with small ponds where we could search for tadpoles, frogs, toads, and newts. Sometimes tadpoles and baby newts would be brought home to rear in tubs of water in our back yards and to our credit we always ensured that once they were mature, we returned them to the meadow. It was an interesting bike ride along the canal tow path to Netherton. In our naivety we believed that the canal water there must be cleaner than in Bootle so in the warm weather we would often go for a swim. A visit to Balliol Road baths was always a popular activity and we would set off to walk there with our swimming costumes wrapped in our rolled-up towels. The baths had two pools, one for boys and one for girls, although at certain times mixed bathing was allowed. Changing room space was limited and at busy times in the boy's pool you had to change on the spectator gallery which had a tarpaulin which could be lowered for decency's sake. Some joker would often try to lower the tarpaulin, which was secured with a rope, and try to catch some boys in the buff. Clothes were put in a wire basket and simply left on the balcony. One time as we dressed to go home one of our group discovered that his trousers had disappeared leaving him to face the lengthy walk home with his wet towel wrapped around his waist We were all very excited to learn one November that a brand-new swimming pool opened in Crosby by the beach. It was an amazing prospect with a huge pool and an enormous diving board. Very quickly we made plans to go and a large group of us walked the several miles carrying our "cosies" in rolled up towels as usual. We gazed at the new pool through the enormous picture window it featured and could not wait to get into the water. We approached the reception desk to pay only to be stopped by a member of staff who asked us where we were from. We replied "Bootle" and to our dismay and astonishment were promptly told to clear off! Greatly offended by this blatant discrimination and burning with a sense of injustice we made our way home. But we had learned our lesson and when we returned the following week and were asked the same question by another staff member we politely and brightly replied "Crosby". We had a fine time in the new pool swimming and showed off jumping off the high diving boards all the while surrounded by residents of Crosby who had no idea that they were sharing their sparkling state of the art pool with a bunch of scallywags from Bootle!

The harsh winter of 1962 – 63 was very memorable. It was the coldest winter on record and the bad weather lasted until well into early spring, perhaps not the best time to be living in a house with little heating or hot water, no insulation, and an outside toilet. I think we must have been made of sterner stuff in those days because I cannot remember complaining too much about the cold. It did not keep us children in, we continued to play outdoors from early in the morning until well after dark, but it did change the nature of our activities. Snowball fights, sledging and creating slides from long stretches of icy road were all great fun. Enterprising as always, we formed work gangs to clear paths and pavements in return for a small contribution from the residents in the street. This was hard work as the snow and ice had frozen as hard as stone. Dressed in our warmest clothes, balaclavas and wellies and armed with lump hammers, pickaxes and shovels we would smash the ice and snow and pile it into heaps in the gutters – piles of ice that remained there until the spring. Eventually all the paths in the street were clear and the pavements right up to the shops in Peel Road were safe to walk on, much to the relief, in particular, of the elderly residents in the street. I remember one occasion that winter when a group of us walked all the way to Netherton on the canal which was frozen solid. In places children had tried to break holes in the ice to reach the water for reasons best known to themselves – perhaps they had ambitions of ice fishing – but the ice was too thick. It was quite a sad sight to see groups of forlorn ducks and geese sliding on the ice in search of a free stretch of water. Another time we walked to Seaforth shore to see the extremely rare sight of frozen sea water washing onto the sand. It certainly was a winter to remember but a huge downside to this was that all football matches were abandoned until March.

All in all, we ranged far and wide, often being out all day and there is no doubt that we were given far more freedom than most parents will allow their children in present times. Were we any safer? Given that we were rarely alone and often in a larger group of mixed aged children then I think we probably were. We also had a resilience and confidence which is often referred to as "street wise" which came from experience in interacting with a large number of young people, some of whom you did your best to avoid, a feeling of safety in numbers and knowing that we always could rely on the support of our friends.

Chapter Seven Church

"Hail Glorious St. Patrick dear saint of our Isle"

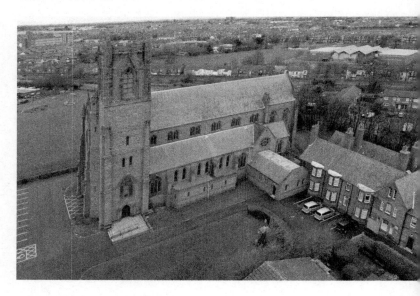

St. James' Church. The Bootle Cathedral.

Most people I knew in the street were Catholics and had Irish surnames. The two closest Catholic churches were St. Joan's on Peel Road and St. James' Church on Chestnut Grove off Marsh Lane although there was an Anglican church St. Leonard's on Bibby's Lane. St Joan of Arc Church was a modern building completed in 1961, the original wooden church having burnt down in 1958. St. James is a huge church which was often referred to as the Bootle Cathedral. A magnificent Gothic Revival church completed in 1886, which could accommodate a thousand worshippers, it dominates the skyline and can be seen from miles away. We attended St. James and my siblings, and I attended the primary school associated with it. The Catholic religion was an important part of our lives. Attendance at Sunday Mass was a necessary part of the day and we accepted as fact, what the nuns at school had drilled into us, that to miss mass was a mortal sin that meant we would go straight to Hell if we were unfortunate enough to die before we could be forgiven in Confession. We wore our "Sunday best" for mass and attended as a family. In those days the priest faced the altar with his back to the congregation and the mass was in Latin, of which I knew very little. It all seemed very mystical but was strangely soothing with its familiar rituals and prayers. There was a lot of physical activity, standing up, kneeling down but not much sitting down apart from during the sermon. This could last some time and was the only bit in the vernacular apart from some of the hymns. The priest, usually Irish, would ascend the elaborate pulpit and deliver his address which usually focussed on all the things we should not be doing if we wanted to avoid an eternity in Hell. We were left in no doubt that this was a fate we should avoid at all costs. In Hell the poor souls, howling in anguish, would be roasted in flames, and tormented by devils who would constantly remind them of what they were missing in Heaven. To reinforce the point parts of the magnificent stained-glass windows in the church portrayed just such scenes. It was all quite intimidating for a young child like me feeling guilty about any recent misdemeanours. Even if you managed to avoid Hell the chances were, unless you were as sinless as one of the saints, that you would have to spend some time in Purgatory atoning for all the venal sins (less than mortal) that you were guilty of. Purgatory was as bad as Hell with one exception – it was not eternal and eventually when cleansed of sin you would be let through the Pearly Gates of Heaven. This was scary stuff, but the Catholic Church was nothing if not fair. Sinners in Purgatory could gain remission if people on Earth prayed for them. This is behind the Catholic tradition of having masses said for loved ones who have passed away which is still widely followed today. In the past the Church sold indulgences so you could bank some remission in advance – a lucrative trade for the clergy. The game changer though was Confession. To our great relief we learned that a visit to the confessional could wipe your soul clean of all your sins. If you did something truly awful like in a fit of homicidal mania you had slaughtered a bus full of nuns, or far, far worse, missed Sunday Mass or eaten meat on a Friday, then a trip to confession put you in the clear and meant you could avoid Hell or a long time in Purgatory. (This is only partly in jest as, after all, remembering the Sabbath day is the third commandment while thou shall not kill comes in only at number five!). This seemed eminently fair to me although, as we were told, you had to be really sorry and repent your sin. The only worry was that if you were run over by a bus before you could get to confession then you were in trouble, but I suppose that was a chance you took. At the end of the day, you always had a choice, as the nuns told us, between doing right or wrong. If you had any confusion between the two concepts, then again, our religion stepped in to help. The nuns taught us that a devil sat on our left shoulder constantly whispering in our ears to do the wrong thing but on our right shoulder our Guardian Angel would be urging us to do the right thing. Simple – all we had to do was listen to our Guardian Angel – genius. I often wondered why so many people chose to ignore their angel. It often occurred to me that the nuns and priests, although doing a splendid job of portraying

Hell and Purgatory as places you would not want to end up in, did not really make much of an effort in selling the attributes of Heaven. To be in Heaven was to be in the presence of God they told us, but they were rather vague in describing the details of what this would be like. We were left in absolutely no doubt what awaited us in Hell but in Heaven? Did this mean we would be in some sort of celestial Butlin's, an eternal holiday with lots of fun activities like fairgrounds, lots of games and activities and all you could eat and drink like hot dogs, Pepsi Cola, ice cream and sweets? Unfortunately, on this the nuns had little to say other than we would be in the presence of God. I began to suspect that the nuns and priests did not really know what went on in Heaven. To be honest sitting round all day for ever, even if it was in the presence of the Almighty, did not really cut it for me, although I supposed, on balance, it beat burning and being tormented by demons.

My sister and I in our Sunday best.

On Sundays we would attend morning mass as a family and we would dress in our best clothes, our "Sunday Best". As we were receiving communion, we had to skip breakfast as you had to fast before receiving the sacrament but after mass Dad usually took us to visit his mother, our Granny. Sadly, my grandfather had died when I was a small child and I hardly remembered him. Granny was a gentle, quietly spoken person and very different to our Mum's mother, our Gran. She lived on Litherland Road in the shadow of the gas works with its huge storage tanks. Granny was extremely house proud and kept her house like a little palace waging a constant battle to keep the aroma of gas from seeping into the house. She was intelligent and a very devout Catholic. A volunteer in her local church she would arrange the flowers on the altar and as she was an accomplished seamstress, she would make the elaborate vestments worn by the priests. Unusual for the time, Granny travelled abroad and after a visit to Rome she presented me with a beautiful child's violin. I drove my family mad as I scratched the bow across the strings producing horrific screeching sounds. After a week the violin mysteriously disappeared never to be seen again. Granny's house also boasted a piano in the parlour although I can never remember anyone actually playing it. An excellent cook she would serve us a tasty, cooked breakfast which we wolfed down after our long fast and this would keep us going until Sunday lunch which Mum would be at home preparing. We always looked forward to this lunch and it never varied – roast chicken, roast potatoes, peas and carrots followed by chocolate cake or ice cream and bananas and if we were lucky a shandy to wash it down. To us kids, perennially hungry, Sunday was an oasis of epicurean delight in the week. After lunch we would dress in our usual street clothes and then play out for the rest of the day.

At school we were prepared by the nuns, teachers, and occasional visits by the priest, for the various sacraments. In fact, we spent a good deal of our time in school on religious matters. The school day began with morning prayers, ended with prayer and in between at noon as the church bells tolled, we would stop what we were doing to say the Angelus. Religious doctrine commenced when we began school and continued thereafter. We were taught how to make the sign of the cross, say our prayers, what the mass meant and told tales of the saints and martyrs, most of whom suffered horrible deaths which gave us nightmares, as inspiration. I particularly remember the story of poor old St. Sebastian who was punished for his faith by the Romans. He was tied to a tree and shot through with arrows. In the horrific picture the nuns showed us he looked like a human pin cushion. We were astonished to learn that he actually survived this ordeal only to be captured once more and then clubbed to death - talk about bad luck. Whenever I thought I was the victim of bad luck I thought of St. Sebastian and quickly realised that things could be a lot worse. The liturgical year was followed, and the significance of the various milestones explained. This began of course with the birth of Jesus at Christmas. Visits to church were regular. In February we attended church to celebrate the feast day of Saint Blaise of Sebaste who miraculously saved a boy chocking to death on a fish bone. In a special ceremony we knelt at the altar and the priest placed two candles, formed in a v shape, across our throats and whispered a blessing. The nuns assured us that this would protect us from all diseases of the throat but, given the number of children who suffered from sore throats and had their tonsils removed, I'm not sure how effective it actually was. To be fair it seemed to work for me, and I can only recall having a sore throat once in my life. On Ash Wednesday we attended a service during which we would go to the altar rail to have an ash cross drawn on our foreheads by the priest. We were told it was a sin to rub this off and in those less hygiene obsessed times, the ash would still be visible on some children for a long time afterwards. The ash was produced from the burnt remains of the palms that were used to decorate the church on Palm Sunday the year before. This event marked the beginning of Lent when we were urged to fast or give up something like sweets for the six-week period. The money we saved from this act of selfless sacrifice was usually put in the red box for oversees missionaries which most homes had and was collected regularly by an order of nuns who wore very elaborate head dresses. My Dad usually gave up alcohol and would not have a beer for the whole period. He would also try to give up smoking but found this more difficult, although in later years gave it up altogether turning instead to eating bags of sweets. During Lent we celebrated St. Patrick's Day. Given that we were taught by Irish head mistresses and most of our priests were Irish then you would expect that the day was regarded as very important. We were all given shamrock to pin on our clothes and a special mass was held in the church and we would be told stories of Patrick's great achievements and the miracles he performed like driving snakes out of Ireland. We sang the hymn "Hail Glorious St. Patrick, dear saint of our Isle". In fact, you would be forgiven for thinking that we lived in Ireland. It was something of a revelation to me to realise, eventually, that we actually lived in England.

We had to attend mass on Good Friday which was always a gloomy celebration marking as it did the Crucifixion. Easter followed three days later and marked the end of Lent, and the nuns did their best to persuade us that this was the greatest celebration of the year. We were not convinced because although it was pleasurable to receive chocolate eggs this could not compare with the presents and excitement of Christmas. Easter Sunday was traditionally the time you put on your new summer clothes, if your parents could afford them. The Easter Sunday dinner was usually a special roast dinner and hopefully Easter Monday Bank Holiday involved a family day out, although this depended on the football fixtures. Not much happened on the religious front then until Advent and the approach of Christmas, apart from the usual round of Sunday Mass and confession although we celebrated innumerable saints' days, many of the saints I had never heard of.

The nuns, teachers and priests prepared us carefully for the various sacraments. The first sacrament was baptism and Catholic babies were traditionally baptised at the earliest opportunity, often just days old. This was to guard against dying without being a member of the Church which meant you could not go to Heaven. According to the Church all babies are born with Original Sin which stems from Adam and Eve's sin of disobedience in Eden when they ate the forbidden fruit. This always struck me as being grossly unfair – why should I, or all babies for that matter, be blamed for Adam and Eve's apple scrumping all those years ago? The only way to be cleansed of Original Sin was to be baptised. If not and the worst happened then a baby's soul went to Limbo, a strange place as I understood it which although not Heaven was not Hell or Purgatory either. I just had this image of a huge nursery full of thousands of babies just lying around doing not much at all for ever and ever. What a very strange idea. No wonder parents wanted their babies baptised as soon as possible.

The first sacrament we were prepared for in school

was Confirmation. This was meant to reinforce our baptism and confirm our membership of the Church. It involved a good deal of preparation in school and then culminated in an elaborate Church service when we were given an additional confirmation name. I chose my brother's name John, and he took me to the ceremony as my Mum was ill at the time and my Dad was working. Following Confirmation, we then prepared for our first confession and communion. This again involved endless preparation in school and church. Confession was quite daunting and when the time came, we sat in a row in church waiting our turn to enter the confessional box – a tiny space with two doors, one door for the priest and one for us sinners. The priest would already be in place and was separated from you by a partition with a small grill to speak through. You could just about make out the priest's face through the grill and it was all quite scary. "Bless me father for I have sinned. It has been two weeks since my last confession and here are my sins", although the bit about the time since your last confession was omitted for your first time. You then had to list all the sins you had committed. Now the nuns had given us clear guidance on this, and it seemed to me that they regarded most things as sinful but even so I genuinely had to wrack my brain for something to confess, after all I didn't want to bore the poor priest who I always suspected was half asleep anyway. If only I had a bank robbery or horrible murder to confess – that would liven things up. But no. I had to resort to owning up about being cheeky to my parents or not doing my homework or forgetting to say my prayers at night. I am sure the priest found it all regrettably mundane. He then said the words to absolve you of your sins and gave you a penance. Mine always seemed to be three Hail Mary's and an Our Father, which was no particular hardship. I often pondered what penance he would give if I had robbed a bank or murdered someone! Once our sins were forgiven, we were in a state of grace and deemed worthy of receiving communion. The nuns made it crystal clear that Holy Communion was a great blessing. We practised endlessly for it and the nuns would use pieces of ice cream wafers to represent the Host which, according to Catholic doctrine, is the actual body of Christ. This was a difficult concept for young minds to take in, but we were terrified of actually dropping the Host on the floor as the nuns made it clear that this would be showing unforgiveable disrespect to Jesus. Eventually the great day dawned, and I was dressed in short dark trousers and a spotless white shirt with a blue sash attached adorned with holy medals. Girls wore elaborate white communion dresses with veils and resembled young brides. Outside church we paraded round the grounds singing hymns before attending a special mass and kneeling at the altar rail to receive communion. In those days the priest placed the Host directly on your tongue and I was conscious of having to stick my tongue out as far as it would go before with a quick "Body of Christ" (in Latin of course) from the priest the job was done. It surprised me that the Host tasted just like the ice cream wafers we had used for practice – I don't know what I expected. This was all witnessed by a church full of proud parents and relatives as First Holy Communion is regarded as a major milestone in a young person's life. With my Mum's ongoing health problems and my Dad's shift work I only had my older sister with me. I was seven years old, and she was nine but what she lacked in years she more than made up for in common sense and ingenuity. On the way home we called into every shop on Marsh Lane and my sister showed off her little brother in his communion clothes and we returned home with a bag of sweets and chocolate donated by the friendly shopkeepers.

Chapter Eight School

"Build a bonfire, build a bonfire put the teachers on the top"

My first school picture. I am first left on the back row.

My first school class photograph shows a group of young children dressed in a range of clothes as we did not seem to be required to wear uniform in reception. In truth, with one or two exceptions (which did not include me) most of the children do not look as if they come from prosperous homes. St. James' School was brick built and typical of the Victorian Board Schools built in the late 19th. Century after the Elementary Education Act 1870 (the Forster Act) which made elementary education compulsory for all.

It was a dark and gloomy building with little in the way of facilities. When I tell people that we learned to write on slate boards I can tell that most do not believe me – but it is true. Until you could form your letters you were not given pencil and paper. In later year groups we began to use pen and ink. This was a messy business which involved using a wooden pen with a nib that had to be dipped constantly into an ink pot which was set into a recessed hole in the desk. The ink was made from powder that had to be mixed with water in a large jug and this was then poured into the individual ink pots. This was a complicated process fraught with potential mishap and it was only entrusted to carefully selected ink monitors. Sadly, I was never selected for this role. Writing with the wooden pen was difficult and the nibs quickly became blunt and had to be replaced. When the class was writing, always in silence in those days, all that could be heard was the scratches and screeches as nibs were dragged across the rough writing paper we used. Ink blots were frequent, and ink would end up on the desk, on clothes and of course on fingers. All school pupils had permanently ink stained fingers which was a tangible and visible mark of an education in the 1950s and 60s. Most of the pieces of writing we produced looked for all the world as if a spider had fallen into the ink well and then dragged itself across the paper in its agonising death throes. Pink blotting paper was essential to dry pieces of writing and pieces of this could be weaponised by dipping it into the ink and then flicking it with a ruler at your intended target.

School was very different to modern schools with their visually stimulating environments and the creative and imaginative lessons that young people benefit from today. Our classrooms were rather dark with little in the way of displays to brighten and energise the learning environment. We sat in long rows of desks and once seated you very rarely left the seat. Classes were large and numbers of thirty or even more were the norm. Group work was virtually unknown and most teaching was didactic with long instruction and explanation from the teacher – chalk and talk was the norm and rote learning parrot fashion was often employed. We learnt to read with "Janet and John" books which used the "look and say" approach which was quite innovative at the time. This basically involved an approach in which words were repeated sufficiently frequently that children memorised them. Today children use the phonics method which encourages them to decode groups of letters. I have to say that Janet and John books were not very interesting with their stilted diction and middle-class content which failed to resonate with children of my background. In contrast my grandson's school reading book as I write is about a wizard who magics dinosaurs into the present and they proceed to cause hilarious mayhem. I'm not sure what Janet and John would have made of it. "Look Janet. There is a dinosaur." "Yes John. It is a dinosaur." A staple of our English lessons was the book "First Aid in English" which had a blue cover with a white cross on the front. This was an English grammar book which covered vocabulary, spelling, syntax, and everything needed to master the English language. It included exercises and as we progressed through the juniors it was made clear to us that the book contained everything we needed to know if we hoped to pass the Eleven Plus examination in year 4. As well as the preparation for the sacraments we also had to learn the Catechism as part of our religious instruction. Every child was issued with a Catechism which was a doctrinal manual in the form of a book containing questions and answers which had to be memorised. Children were tested on this so if the teacher asked, "Who made you?" the correct response was "God made me." Then came "Why did God make you?" to be answered with "God made me to love and serve him in this life and to be with him for eternity in the next." And so on. It was not really riveting stuff. I vividly remember maths lessons which consisted of chanting out times tables to the rhythm of the teacher hitting the cane on the desk. It worked but my, was it tedious. It amuses me now that due to the encouragement of politicians like Michael Gove, who believe that everything worthwhile lies in the past, times tables are back in a big way in schools. All well and good but then I discovered that children are still required to learn up to times twelve – why not times ten or thirteen or fourteen for that matter? Of course, the reason we went up to times twelve was simply because there were twelve pennies in a shilling, so this is hardly a requirement in these days of decimal coinage. History lessons invariably involved learning long lists of kings and queens with the dates of their reigns and how the British Empire was forged and how beneficial it was to the millions of people it was forced upon. This was reinforced in geography lessons when we gazed at a world map covered in red which proved that the Sun never set on the Empire. Of course, this was an outdated concept even then as Empire gave way to Commonwealth but still, we were left in no doubt how superior the British were to lesser peoples and how to be born an Englishman was to win first prize in the lottery of life as Cecil Rhodes had claimed. I often think that this view, in which we were indoctrinated, sowed the seeds for my generation's support for Brexit. I particularly remember music lessons. This consisted of sitting round a large loudspeaker set into a large piece of polished wood which was connected to the wireless. We were given song sheets and then the teacher would tune in to the BBC schools' service and the "Singing Together" programme. Along with thousands of other children up and down the country we would then belt out songs together with the singers on the wireless. At the top of our lungs, we would sing traditional songs like "Hearts of Oak", "The British Grenadiers", "The Raggle Taggle Gypsy", "The Skye Boat Song" and "D'ye ken John Peel". Another programme was "Music and Movement" when the presenter would issue instructions like "Now children we are going to sway like trees in the wind," after which we would stand and wave our arms in the air. We must have looked quite mad! My favourite lessons were sport and PE. At first PE was very traditional as we stood in lines and performed a range of physical activities that children in the !800s would be familiar with. Later the school purchased a set of equipment that included ropes and wall bars that made lessons more challenging and interesting. Games usually involved running, cricket or football games undertaken in the school yard – the school had no outside green space. In the juniors in year 3 and 4 (years 5 and 6 in the new money) we had football on Stuart Road playing fields off Southport Road which was almost two miles from the school. This took a whole afternoon as we walked there and back and after changing, we just about had time for a game. We walked crocodile fashion with our boots strung around our necks and our football kit squashed into our boots-nobody had designer kit bags in those days. It was wonderful to play on grass on a proper pitch with white lines and goal nets and we could emulate our heroes at Goodison Park or Anfield. I was not totally useless at football and all those endless hours of playing in the street stood me in good stead as I was chosen for the school team when still in year 3 and then in year 4, I became captain of the team. Matches against our rival schools in Bootle were always very competitive and often watched by small crowds of parents and onlookers. I always smelled of liniment as my Dad was convinced it was essential to warm up the muscles, so he ensured I kept a bottle with my kit and rubbed it on my legs before a game. He always watched me play when his shift work allowed but this was a mixed blessing as he was a harsh critic, convinced as he was that he was something of an authority on the beautiful game. I played at right full back to begin with, and he always stressed the importance of clattering the opposing left winger at the earliest opportunity as this would impose my domination over him. I took him at his word, and I was guilty of some horrendous challenges which gained me a bit of a reputation which followed me through all the years I played competitive football. Nowadays I would be red carded every game! Recently while watching my grandson at football training my son in law and I witnessed a Dad severely reprimanding his young son. "What did he do wrong?" my son in law asked me. I replied, "He did what my Dad always insisted that I did when I was playing!" In year 3 our school shirts were the type with laced collars and the style worn by players of Dixie Dean's era. They were very thick and virtually indestructible and were the self-same shirts worn by my brother when he played for the team ten years before. To my delight in year 4 we were given brand new kit – short sleeves and V necks as worn by England's top teams at the time.

In the juniors we began swimming lessons. This involved another long walk, this time to Balliol Road baths. Lessons were given by an instructor, the teacher accompanying us retiring to an office to drink tea and read the paper. The instructor had a very innovative teaching method which basically consisted of lining us up at the deep end and then pushing in those who failed to jump in on his command. You swam or sunk. He had one of those long poles meant to haul out bathers in trouble but in fact he used this to whack your fingers if you tried to grasp the edge of the pool. Strangely it seemed to work, and I cannot recall anyone not surviving the exercise. I am not sure how this method would be regarded today but I am not aware of anyone thinking it strange at the time.

Sometimes lessons were interrupted by the arrival of the school health service team. In these early days of the National Health Service inspections were regularly carried out to check our general health, our eyesight, our teeth and, of course, our hair. The visit of "Nitty Nora the Jungle Explorer" was not especially welcomed. We were made to line up and the "nit nurse" would sit us down one by one. A thorough inspection was then carried out and if she discovered any evidence of infestation a child would be issued with a white card to inform the parents of what treatment was required. The sense of shame on the faces of those receiving a card was palpable and this could not be concealed from all the other children waiting their turn. I cannot recall failing the "nit nurse's" inspection and this is probably due to Mum's diligence as she never failed to carry out a regular check as my sister and I leant over a sheet of newspaper as Mum carefully dragged a fine-toothed comb through our hair. A far more serious threat to our health was the polio outbreak in the 1950s. The disease mainly affected children and there were 45,000 cases in the UK and hundreds died. For many contracting the disease the symptoms were awful and children suffered paralysis with long periods in an "iron lung" needed to help them breathe and survive. Even then many needed the support of leg callipers to help them walk for many years after. What made it scarier was that little was known about its cause or how it spread. Thankfully a vaccine for polio was developed in the 1950s and I can remember queuing up at a vaccination centre to receive a first jab. Needles were not the very fine instruments we are accustomed to now- they were thicker and longer, and you certainly felt them going in. We were all relieved when we learnt that the second dose could be administered on a sugar cube which was far less traumatic. The vaccination programme was highly effective and polio cases fell rapidly and have since been eliminated in the UK. Even so I can remember several children in my primary school who needed the support of leg callipers after surviving the disease.

Despite the eccentricities of some of the practices of our teachers or instructors we complained about very little and mostly just accepted what we were told or how we were treated. Physical punishment was routine and accepted. The usual punishment was the cane. Every teacher kept one on their desk and some used it more than others. The canes, shaped like walking sticks, were thin and bundles of them would be delivered to the school, along with other supplies, in the large green vans used at the time. Usually, you would be caned on the hand which would be held out at shoulder height to the side. The teacher would then whip the cane across your palm. It hurt – a lot. It was wise to try to bend your thumb down because if the cane caught you across the thumb, it was hugely painful. Physical punishment was often metered out for infringements that would now be regarded as very minor in modern schools. The most extreme punishment was six of the best – three on each hand. It was difficult to disguise the tears that would automatically spring into your eyes as the pain hit you, but it was a mark of honour to try to put on a brave show even if when you sat back down you would surreptitiously sit on your hand to ease the sting. Despite this you could still carry the red welt of the cane on your hand for hours. It never occurred to us to complain about this treatment to our parents because it was likely that they would side with the teacher and punish you themselves for getting into trouble at school. Some teachers were expert at using the cane and I remember one diminutive female teacher who used to take a small jump to add force to her swing. Sometimes teachers would resort to other forms of punishments like slaps or twisting ears or even throwing the wooden board rubber. How very different schools were then. Years later when I became a teacher myself in Liverpool the cane was still being used. Once I finished my probationary year I was issued with a cane and authorised to use it in accordance with the school's discipline policy. I never used it and a few years later physical punishment was banned. I do wish I had kept that cane though as a memento.

Our school building was Victorian, and the facilities were pretty basic. We had no green space, just a large school yard that we were thrown out in no matter what the weather. The toilets were outside in a corner of the yard and the boys' toilet consisted of a large urinal and three stalls. It had no roof and if it rained you got wet. Older boys would compete to try and urinate over the brick walls which enclosed the toilet. The girls knew this and stayed well away from this part of the school yard! There were no sinks in the toilet as these were situated near the cloakroom inside the school building. However, we did receive free school milk. The Free School Milk Act 1945 gave every child under 18 the right to a third of a pint of milk each day, although some local authorities had been providing this service for many years. It came in small bottles and was distributed by the milk monitors, another envied post which I never achieved. In winter the milk was often frozen pushing the tops off the bottles. It would be placed near the radiators to melt but this meant that by the time it was served to us it was tepid and tasted awful. The Conservative Government in a very controversial move in 1971 ended free milk for children over seven years of age. Margaret Thatcher the Secretary of State for Education was for ever after known as "Thatcher the Milk Snatcher" although there is some evidence that she was against the move but it was forced through by the Prime Minister Edward Heath.

As we progressed through the juniors, we concentrated on preparations for the Eleven Plus examination. All children sat this which included tests in English, maths, verbal and non-verbal reasoning.

The result of this examination determined what type of school a young person progressed to. Around a third of pupils passed the examination and secured a place in a grammar school while the majority who failed went on to a secondary modern school. Passing or not passing became a defining moment in a young person's life. A place in grammar school offered a more traditional academic education with the potential of university and a well-paid white-collar occupation. Secondary modern schools offered a more practical curriculum and the more likely progression to a blue-collar job at aged 15. This was controversial even at the time and many felt it wrong to regard children as failures at the tender age of eleven and it was argued that the test was biased in favour of middle-class children. It was phased out by the Labour Government in the 1960's as comprehensive schools were introduced but a version of the test is still used in those areas that have retained grammar schools like the Wirral. At the time the only Catholic grammar school in our area was St. Mary's College in Crosby. As well as passing the eleven plus to gain entry boys also had to sit the College's own entrance examination. My brother had attended the school and was very successful there gaining "A" levels and progressing on to teacher training college, but he maintained that boys from Bootle were always at a disadvantage compared to those from the more prosperous Crosby. Many of the staff were Christian Brothers and they had a reputation for strict discipline and eccentricity. My brother was good at sport but was disappointed that football was not played at the school as rugby was the main winter sport. He played for the school team and matches were held on Wednesday afternoons although this time was clawed back for academic subjects by way of Saturday morning school. This was an additional headache for my brother as, like his Dad, he was a keen follower of Everton, and this severely restricted his ability to attend away games. He was a good footballer and played for a Sunday League team, but this had to be kept quiet at school because association football was frowned upon by the staff and it may have resulted in him losing his place in the school rugby team. He also disliked the fact that the school blazer was red in colour! All in all, his experience did not leave me with a burning ambition to attend the school. Nevertheless, gaining a place at grammar school was regarded as a major achievement by our primary school and our Dad who was convinced of the value of a good education so I spent a good deal of time in school preparing for the eleven plus and St. Mary's entrance examination. In fact, together with several other boys we were sent to Crosby to sit the examination a year early while in year 3 (year 5 in the new money). The reasoning was that if we passed it we could then concentrate on the eleven plus and if we failed we could sit it again the following year. So, one sunny morning in the summer term of year 3 I met three fellow pupils at the bus stop in Knowsley Road. We had been given very detailed instructions by Sister Cuthbert and we were furnished with pens, pencils, rubber and ruler all wrapped in a rubber band. The big, red Ribble bus dropped us off right outside the school and we made our way up the long school drive. It was very different to our school, with its tree lined drive and lots of green spaces. We were ushered into a large hall with rows and rows of small examination desks. The teachers, or masters as they were known, were either Christian Brothers in their long brown cassocks or lay teachers wearing academic gowns. It was all quite intimidating to four small boys from Bootle. Many of the other boys were from Crosby and some of them had attended the school's preparatory school. We sat in silence as long detailed instructions were read out from the front. Some of it went over my head and when I put my hand up to ask a question a master came over and cuffed me across the ear and told me to listen more carefully. This put me in a great frame of mind for the examination! I cannot recall whether I passed that test because to my great relief a development the following year changed the whole prospective. Unknown to me at the time there were plans afoot for a Catholic grammar school to be established in Bootle run by the Salesian priests of Don Bosco. In my final year of primary school my Dad attended a meeting held by the Salesians and he was mightily impressed. He discovered that they were very keen on sport, particularly football and that they liked a drink. Quite how he discovered this at an introductory meeting I am not too sure, but he could relate to them immediately and regarded them as kindred spirits. Later he would be instrumental in helping to form the school's P.T.A and he became an enthusiastic supporter of the school. Dad came home from this initial meeting and told me to make sure I passed the eleven plus and I could forget about St. Mary's. Despite the pressure of the Eleven Plus examination I thoroughly enjoyed my final year in primary school. Our teacher was Tom O'Connor, and he was fun, friendly and an inspirational teacher. Tom had lived in Spencer Street, as did my brother and although Tom was a couple of years older, they were friends and part of the same street gang. Like my brother he had attended St. James' and then St. Mary's College. He was developing his career as a comedian and entertainer and if we had worked hard during the week our reward came on Friday afternoon. Tom would take out his guitar and we would sing songs and he would practise his night club routine. It was great fun. Tom did not really tell conventional jokes. Rather he was an "observational style" comedian and told funny stories based on his shrewd observations of real life. A group of us were interested in learning guitar and Tom gave us lessons in his own time, often in his own home and his wife Pat would serve us lemonade and biscuits. I still occasionally pick up the guitar, but I can only play songs that contain the four or five chords that Tom taught me all those years ago. Tom moved on to teach music and mathematics at St. Joan of Arc's secondary school and became deputy head teacher. He left teaching after his big break on "The Comedians" and "Opportunity Knocks" television programmes and went on to host a number of game shows, his own "Tom O'Connor" show and was the subject of "This is Your Life" in 1977. I was saddened to learn that he had passed away in July 2021.

Chapter Nine Health Issues

"Doctor, doctor give me the news"

My Dad's instruction to pass the eleven plus was easier said than done because I had something of a difficult time in my final years of primary school. My mother had a number of serious health problems which started when I was eight. She had a stroke when in the hairdresser's and she spent a long time in hospital. She never fully recovered, lost the use of her left arm and was weak down the left side of her body. After this she developed a serious heart condition and underwent heart surgery. This was fairly new practice at the time, and she was given a fifty per cent chance of surviving the operation. She spent another long period of time in hospital following this. This meant that for a long time my sister and I never saw our Mum and, in truth, being the age I was, I more or less forgot her. As my Dad worked shifts and my brother was attending college in Salford, our Gran was drafted in to care for us. She had a very robust view of how to look after children which was probably formed during her own very hard upbringing. I remember her technique of washing me before bed. She would sit me on the draining board with my feet in the sink and then proceed to rub my arms and knees with the scrubbing brush and Life Boy soap. I am convinced that she permanently removed the top layer of my skin! She had it in for my sister. I'm not sure why. Maybe because my sister resembled my Dad's sisters who she was not fond of and also my sister was feisty and not easily subdued. One time when my sister answered her back Gran threw the grill pan at her which fortunately missed taking a chunk out of the wall. Moving in with us did not stop Gran's social life. After she put my sister and me to bed, she would be off to the pub. Of course, as soon as she shut the front door we would be up, dressed, open the bedroom window, and then shin down the drainpipe into the back yard. For the next few hours, we would play in the street and backyard always ensuring we were back in bed by closing time. Then we would wait to hear Gran, accompanied by one or two of her cronies, come walking back down the street singing at the top of their voices. After a short while she would look round the bedroom door to check on us. For some reason, even though the house had electricity, she always carried a candle and with her long grey hair she represented a daunting image. If she guessed we were awake she would wave the candle about and tell us that the Devil would take us away if we didn't get to sleep. This domestic situation became more worrying when our Dad broke his leg while trying to kick start his motor bike. He spent a few weeks in hospital himself and by this time my sister and I felt that we had truly been abandoned. Years later when I was living in Netherton I was on the bottom deck of the last 28 bus from town. I was with my girlfriend (who eventually became my wife). At the Marsh Lane stop several revellers fresh from the Marsh Lane pubs boarded the bus. A couple of elderly women sang and danced between the seats lifting their skirts to show their bloomers. My girlfriend whispered to me "Oh, they are disgusting." I said nothing and stared out of the window trying to be anonymous but to my consternation one of them peered down at me and called out my name. "Hello Gran," I replied! The look on my girlfriend's face was priceless.

Things became more difficult when, some months later, I became really unwell, and I was taken to our GP's surgery on Knowsley Road. I became worse and this time Gran requested a home visit from the doctor. He probably thought I was not too unwell because curiously Gran insisted that I prepared for his visit by being scrubbed clean and sat up in bed looking as healthy and as bright eyed and bushy tailed as I could manage. You were meant to look your best for the doctor in those days! A few days later I collapsed at home and this time the GP summoned an ambulance to rush me off to Alder Hey Hospital. A small crowd gathered in the street to see me stretchered into the ambulance and wave me off and wish me good luck. In hospital the surgeons planned to take out my appendix. After tests, however, and noticing my distinctly yellowed complexion, they found that I had contacted hepatitis A and I was transferred to Olive Mount Isolation Hospital for a lengthy stay of six weeks. Hepatitis A is an infectious disease of the liver and symptoms include nausea, vomiting, diarrhoea, jaundice, fever, and abdominal pain, all of which I had. I was unlucky as younger children can have the disease and yet exhibit little or no symptoms. It is a disease associated with poor sanitation and is usually spread by eating food or drinking water contaminated with infected faeces, although it can be spread through close contact with an infected person. I suspect swimming in the sea by a sewage outlet probably did for me! Olive Mount Children's Hospital was originally sixteen cottage homes erected for pauper children around an existing main house in 1898 in Mill Lane Wavertree. It later became a children's hospital catering for a range of medical conditions. The block I was based in had two isolation wards, one for hepatitis and one for tuberculosis. Visiting was strictly limited to one half hour on a Sunday and only two visitors were allowed. Even then they had to wear protective clothing and footwear and a mask. It was all quite intimidating. I remember that visitors had to walk across a special mat which had a sticky substance covering it, presumably to remove any dirt and bacteria. We had to remain in bed and visitors were not allowed to sit down or touch us. After half an hour a bell would ring, visitors were ushered out quickly and that was it until next Sunday. Any gift of sweets was placed in a small cupboard to be shared out to everyone in the ward and as we were on a fat-controlled diet, we were not allowed chocolate. During the night, together with the bolder members of our ward, I would join a raiding party to invade the TB ward to ransack their sweet cupboard and, of course, our cupboard had to be protected from revenge attacks-it often resulted in lively scuffles and there was always the danger of the night staff catching us in the act and informing Matron. This was something to dread as everyone was terrified of Matron including the doctors and other nursing staff. She ruled with a rod of iron and reminded me of the headmistress nuns in my school. Every morning she would conduct her ward inspection. The nurses would prepare us for this and make sure we were clean and sitting bolt upright in our beds wearing our bed jackets with not a creased sheet in sight. We dared not make a sound as she walked slowly down the ward. Nothing escaped her attention, and you dreaded the thought of her pausing at your bed. I have to say that she looked resplendent in her uniform as did all the nurses at that time and this is quite a contrast to today when everyone, from doctors to cleaners, is dressed in scrubs. Indeed, in some organisations the title of matron has been substituted with "senior clinical nurse manager"! It does not have the same ring to it!

The hospital placed great store on the restorative powers of fresh air and our building had walls that could be rolled back to allow fresh air to flood the ward. There was a small play area and park outside and we were encouraged to get out of bed and go to play outside. Sadly, the concept of education was not forgotten, and the hospital service employed teachers to provide basic lessons. We even had practical lessons when we were taught how to weave baskets which we could give to our families as presents. My Dad sent in Airfix kits which kept me busy, and I constructed a number of military planes like the Sopwith Camel and Spitfire. This was useful because they came in a plastic bag which I could then use to pour in the disgusting sterilised milk they insisted we drank and throw it out the window. Unfortunately, they discovered my deception when one day a bag hit one of the gardeners and he informed Matron. She made sure that one of the nurses stood guard while I drank my milk in future.

We were made to bathe each day in a huge bath which could accommodate several small boys. Privacy was an unknown concept and even the toilet bowls were in a row with no cubicles to protect your dignity but at least you could have a good chat while sitting on your throne. Eventually I began to feel better and looked forward to being discharged. After six weeks one of the doctors examined me and declared that I could go home the following Saturday. Luckily my Dad was not working that day and confirmed that he could come to take me home.

Unfortunately, it was also FA Cup Final Day, and this meant I had to wait until after the game which he was watching on TV. I waited anxiously in my own clothes in the nurses' office until about five thirty when there was a tremendous racket outside as my Dad arrived on his motorbike to take me home. Matron was not on duty thank goodness, but a row followed between my Dad and the Staff Nurse who could not believe that I was to travel home on the back of a motorbike and initially refused to let me go. Eventually she gave in, probably keen to see the back of my Dad rather than being convinced of my welfare, and so it was that I returned to Wordsworth Street, windswept and cold but glad to be home.

Chapter Ten Entertainment

"Sing something simple as time goes by"

Despite my Mum's illness and long absence home life was very happy. My Dad was a real character and fun to be around and my sister and I were very fond of our elder brother. He was very popular, had lots of friends and he had a great sense of fun. He kept us entertained, playing his guitar, telling jokes and funny stories and doing impersonations. If a Buddy Holly song came on the wireless, he would rush and put on his special "Buddy" glasses and sing along. If it was an Elvis song, he would quiff his hair, turn up his collar, curl his lip and sing along with the "King". Despite our age difference I got on very well with my older brother. We shared a room for several years and at night he would tell me stories. My favourite was about a superhero called Superman who I thought was a real person for quite a time. Later I retained my interest and built up quite a collection of D.C. comics and I became quite an expert on the exploits of Batman, Green Lantern, the Flash, and the other superheroes in the D.C. world. One Christmas a relative bought me a Subbuteo table football game and I quickly developed a great enthusiasm for the game. So did my brother and unfortunately the game brought out the worst in our competitive spirits. We played regularly and when my brother purchased a small silver cup to play for each week the intensity of the games increased – think of the passion of the Old Firm games between Rangers and Celtic and treble it! I never thought that you could sustain injuries playing table football! These games lasted for years even after my brother married and had his first child. When my girlfriend and I went to baby sit my brother would drive his wife Pat mad because they would invariably set off late because our hotly disputed match would often need extra time and even penalties to decide the winner!

We did not have a television at first and the wireless was our main form of entertainment. It was kept in the kitchen, which was our family room, and was a treasured possession. Wireless sets were expensive and not all families could afford one. Ours was a splendid item made by Bush. It had a wooden effect Bakelite case with a cream panel through which the sound emerged and below this was a black tuning dial which listed the stations you could tune into by twisting one of the three white knobs. One of the knobs adjusted the volume while the other switched between long wave and medium wave. The tuning dial indicated a number of exotic stations such as Lille, Warsaw, Allouis and Luxembourg although in truth we only listened to the BBC stations. The Light Programme featured popular music as well as mainstream entertainment such as sport, variety shows, comedy and drama. The Home Service had some general entertainment programmes and more serious drama but was the main channel for news. The Third Programme only broadcast in the evening and was highbrow in character featuring classical music and talks on a range of topics. Needless to say, we rarely tuned into this programme. The wireless was plugged into the mains and had valves which took a little while to warm up. The tuning dial was lit and this made for cosy listening in the evenings, with the big room light switched off and the coal fire flickering away adding to the atmosphere. You used your imagination to create pictures in your mind to accompany the drama you were listening to – watching television is a much more passive activity. The wireless was a constant soundtrack to home life. My Mum loved "Housewives' Choice", "Music while you Work" and "Mrs. Dale's Diary". In the evening band shows were always popular and there were some excellent dramas like "Dick Barton Special Agent" and comedians like Arthur Askey, who was a Scouser, and Tommy Trinder. "Educating Archie" was popular although it never occurred to us how odd it was to feature a ventriloquist act on the radio. We really enjoyed "The Clitheroe Kid" starring Jimmy Clitheroe and his mad cap antics. On Sundays "Two Way Family Favourites" was broadcast opening with its theme of "With a Song in My Heart". Hosted by

Cliff Michelmore and Jean Metcalfe, it was a request programme designed to link families at home with British Forces serving overseas. It made me sad when the request usually ended with a phrase like "looking forward to you coming home in" and then a date often several years in the future! At lunch time there were some excellent comedy shows like "The Navy Lark", "Hancock's Half Hour" and "Beyond Our Ken". Later in the afternoon "Sing Something Simple" featuring The Cliff Adams Singers was popular and my parents often joined in singing the popular songs that were the staple diet of the programme. In those days everything was suitable for family listening with not a swear word to be heard. There were some programmes designed for younger listeners. Pre-school children enjoyed "Listen with Mother" a short afternoon slot which consisted of a short story, a nursery rhyme and a song. School age children had "Children's Hour" from 5 to 6 pm. It had a variety of content including informative features on a range of subjects, music and serialisations such as "Jennings at School" and the "Just so Stories". On Saturday mornings it was "Children's Favourites" hosted by "Uncle Mac". The songs played did not feature in the charts but rather were established favourites like "The Ugly Duckling", "The Runaway Train", "Nellie the Elephant" and the rather sinister "Sparky the Magic Piano". There was something magical about listening to the wireless which I sometimes think that television fails to capture. I still like listening to the radio and especially enjoy tuning into football commentaries when a skilful commentator can sometimes create a more compelling account of the action than that provided by the picture box in the corner.

Of course, like most families we eventually purchased our first television set. I remember when the first family in the street installed a television. We kids stood in the street and watched with great interest as a man climbed a ladder up to the roof and attached a large H shaped aerial to the chimney stack. The family in question were kind enough to cram all their children's friends into their parlour to watch "Children's Hour" after school and this continued for quite a while until eventually other families purchased their own sets. Our first set was installed in the kitchen next to the wireless and it was quite a significant purchase as television sets were expensive and could only be afforded by buying on "the never never" as hire purchase was often referred to. Our TV had a walnut wooden surround and stood on four spindly legs. The screen was much smaller than the huge wide screen TVs popular today and the picture was black and white and a much lower resolution than modern sets, but we were very proud of it. There were only two channels BBC and ITV but a third channel BBC2 was introduced in 1964. There were many popular programmes. Mum's favourite on Sunday was "Dr. Finlay's Casebook" or "Bookcase" as she called it and she loved "Perry Mason" starring Raymond Burr shown during the week. "Z Cars" was popular based in the fictional town of Newtown but we Scousers all knew that it was really Kirkby. That programme and "Coronation Street" were unusual in that the characters spoke like we did which was very different to the posh cut glass BBC accent we were used to hearing on the wireless and TV. There were many excellent American comedies like "Bewitched", "The Beverley Hillbillies" and "Mr. Ed" the talking horse. Like many movies they showed us a world very different to ours with homes that had central heating, multiple bathrooms and luxury kitchens with dishwashers! My brother particularly liked programmes that I could only watch from behind the sofa and sometimes with my eyes closed. "The Twilight Zone", "Quatermass and the Pit" and "Dr. Who" featuring the Daleks were really scary at the time and could give you nightmares. It was safer to watch the programmes made for younger audiences such as "Animal Magic" with Johnny Morris providing the humorous voices for a range of animals. "Blue Peter" and "Crackerjack" were favourites of mine. I always envied those who had a Blue Peter Badge. John Noakes was a real live action man who was ready for any challenge and, in later years, broke the record for the longest free-fall parachute jump for a British civilian. I still think the time when Lulu the baby elephant from London Zoo visiting the programme went rogue, defecated on the set and then dragged its keeper through the mess, is one the funniest sequences ever shown on TV. John and his co-presenters Val Singleton and Peter Purvis were helpless with laughter in this live broadcast. "Crackerjack" with Leslie Crowther, Peter Glaze and the excellent game "Double or Drop" was essential viewing and yes, I did yell "Crackerjack!" back at the screen every time the word was mentioned. Having a TV was a great luxury and made for many cosy family evenings with the lights switched off and the only other illumination being the flickering light from the coal fire.

As wonderful as we thought television was, however, it could not compete with a visit to the pictures. There were several cinemas in Bootle at that time and, of course, in Liverpool city centre. My Dad was a keen cinema goer and would take my sister and me to the pictures as a treat. Our local cinema was the Bootle Odeon on Stanley Road just opposite the Broadway Stores. The "Broadie", as we referred to it, was a place of wonder and fascination to us kids. It sold all sorts of things you could not get anywhere else. It had yellow transparent blinds to protect its window displays from the sun and we would sometimes walk there just to look at the goods on display. It sold a range of gifts and ornaments but, of more interest to us, it also sold toys, model railways, aircraft, cars and other items that we craved. For instance, during the craze for yoyos it stocked "Lumar 99s" which were top of the range models highly sort after. The store sold high quality catapults fitted with donkey rubber which could be lethal if loaded with a glass marble. We purchased our "spud guns" there, which were great fun and then later our "Gat" air guns which fired .177 lead pellets and corks. The store assistants wore blue overall coats and would sell us our air gun pellets without a murmur. It really was an Aladdin's Cave full of everything children desired. As I write I am pleased to say that the store is still trading, looks almost the same but probably no longer sells air guns! We would walk to the Odeon and with a bit of luck Dad would buy us a Pepsi and a hotdog. I cannot remember whether it was in place when I was a child but years later, when we lived in our first house near Linacre Mission, my wife and I would go to the pictures on Sunday evenings and often have a hotdog in the interval. We were fascinated because the assistant would place one hotdog at a time into a small slot in this huge metal contraption which would make a very loud humming noise. A minute later a piping hot dog would be extracted. "Is that an oven?" we asked, only to be informed that it was in fact a microwave oven, the first of its kind we had seen. Even after the assistant tried to explain how it worked, we were still none the wiser! Dad took us to see some wonderful movies like "One Hundred and One Dalmatians". "Peter Pan", "Swiss Family Robinson" and "The Adventures of Huckleberry Finn". On Saturday mornings a gang of us kids would walk to the pictures as we were members of the Odeon Saturday Morning Club. The cinema would be packed with children, and it was absolute bedlam. With hindsight I feel great sympathy for the poor usherettes whose job it was to keep things orderly – an impossible task. The session began with the club song with the words shown on the screen – but we didn't need them. We would belt out the song at the top of our lungs – "We come along on Saturday mornings greeting everybody with a smile." Then followed a programme of short films like a "Mighty Mouse" or "Atom Ant" cartoon after which a longer film, usually a serial like "The Lone Ranger" or my favourite "Flash Gordon". Flash was a great hero who battled evil cosmic villains helped by Dr. Zarkov and the beautiful Dale Arden. I particularly enjoyed the episodes featuring the Emperor Ming who ruled the planet Mongo. Dale Arden was the heroine but we all secretly reserved our affection for Ming's daughter the Princess Aura who seemed eminently more exotic to our eyes. There was absolutely no convention of silence during the movie as there was with an adult audience. We cheered the heroes and booed the bad guys and often things would be hurled at the screen.

Episodes always ended with a cliff hanger, for example with Flash clinging desperately onto a spaceship as his fingers slipped and he fell into the abyss. To a background of dramatic music, a commanding voice would ask if Flash could survive and urge us to be sure to watch the next episode to find out. We would be on tenterhooks all week only to return the following Saturday to discover that, in fact, we must have only imagined that Flash's fingers had slipped off because it appeared that at the last moment, he had managed to swing his legs up and get a firmer grip on the rocket's tail fin and so save himself. What a relief! It never occurred to us to question the integrity of this ruse, even though something similar happened every week, because after all it was great fun. There was normally an interval on Saturday mornings and one of the staff would come onto the stage and bring on those celebrating birthdays. Sometimes there were events like yoyo or hula hoop competitions. One time the Corona lemonade company sponsored a colouring competition. A street scene of a van delivering lemonade was distributed and entries were handed in the following week. The next Saturday I was amazed to be called up onto the stage to discover I had won second place and a few days after that my prize was delivered to our house by a Corona van – eight bottles of lemonade. I felt really guilty because in fact I had asked my older brother to colour in the entry and he was not an Odeon Club member! Nevertheless, I thoroughly enjoyed the lemonade which was a rare treat.

Chapter Eleven Wolf Cubs

"Akela we'll do our best"

Many children in those days joined the local scout or cub group, although some boys preferred the Boys' Brigade. My brother was a scout in the Bootle 10th Scout Group which was based in the church hall in Hooton Place, just off Chestnut Grove. He was a very keen member of the troop, taking part in the annual camps and he was in the scout band. At first, he played the bugle, and I can picture him now on Church Parade Sundays each month marching down Marsh Lane, his cheeks bulging as he blasted out the tune. Later he was promoted to drums which allowed him to make just as much noise but with far less effort. Following in his footsteps I joined as a Wolf Cub as we were known then. The Wolf Cubs had been founded by Lord Baden-Powell for boys too young to become scouts and it derived much of its terminology from "The Jungle Book" written by Baden-Powell's friend Rudyard Kipling. Everything a cub needed to know was set out in "The Wolf Cub's Handbook". Being a member of the pack was great fun and we played lots of games and learnt lots of
126

new skills. I loved the uniform which consisted of a navy-blue jersey, a blue and yellow neckerchief kept in place by a leather woggle with a wolf's head image and a green cricket cap with yellow strips. The cap had a wolf's head image and as you progressed you could add first one star and then a second star. The uniform was quite distinct, and I was very proud to wear it. After you joined the pack, you were invested as a Tenderpad as soon as you had learnt the cub motto of "Do your best" and the wolf cub promise – "I promise to do my best, to do my duty to God and the Queen, to keep the law of the Wolf Cub Pack and to do a good turn to somebody every day." You could then progress after time to the first star which was awarded after you had demonstrated various knowledge and skills such as how to colour the Union Jack and how to hang it correctly. It still amuses me to see the flag hung upside down by self-proclaimed British nationalists and Olympic athletes amongst others. I once caused quite a stir whilst on holiday in a Spanish hotel when I pointed out to the manager that they had our flag the wrong way up. You also had to know the first and third verse of the National Anthem (I'm not sure what was wrong with the second verse) and how to tie a number of knots including the famous reef knot. Things became more interesting when working towards the second badge when you had to swim 50 yards, learn how to set a compass and, best of all, cook sausages over a campfire! As you learnt new skills you were awarded with badges which could be sewn on your jersey. As time went on and if you were industrious, the jersey would be covered in badges. Tying knots was an essential skill as was lighting a campfire and erecting a tent. There were badges for cooking, sport and animal tracking. There was even a badge for making a telephone call, the opportunity for which had never presented itself to most of us. Nobody in our street had a home telephone. After a few practice sessions Akela would take us to a nearby phone box to be assessed for the badge. In turn we would lift the receiver, feed in four pennies, press button A to drop the coins, dial the number we had been given and then as Akela's husband answered the phone, we would press button B to be connected. It was a complicated business but if we managed it we were assured of our badge. Eventually I was the proud owner of a jersey covered in badges. Wolf cub packs were divided into groups of six boys known as "sixes". The leader of the six known as the "sixer" had two yellow stripes on the arm of his jersey and his assistant the "seconder" had one. I worked my way up to both positions and after a few years I became the senior member of the pack, the "senior sixer", and had three yellow stripes. Our weekly meetings began with The Grand Howl when we would form a circle around Akela and her helper Baloo. We would crouch down like wolf cubs and on a signal would shout out "Akela we will do our best" to which she would respond "You will dyb, dyb, dyb" (Do your best) as we shot up and performed the two fingered salute. We would then drop our right hand as we shouted out "We will dob, dob, dob" (Do our best). The two fingered salute was meant to represent a wolf cub's ears, but I suspect that its other interpretation is the reason that cubs now use the scouts' three fingered version. Years later I was in Costa Coffee in the Albert Dock with my wife, daughter, and grandchildren. It was very busy, and a cub scout group came in searching for seats. The cub scout leader and his assistant asked if they could sit in the spare seats on our table. We began talking and I was interested to know how cub scouting had changed. I asked if The Grand Howl was still practised, and my grandchildren asked me what it was. Without further ado in a packed coffee bar, I demonstrated how it was performed, to the bemusement of the other customers but also the applause of the cub scout group. Once a wolf cub always a wolf cub! I was pleased to discover that they still had woggles!

A highlight of the year for wolf cubs was "Bob-a-Job Week". Cubs and scouts would perform various jobs and chores, such as tidying gardens or doing a little shopping for family, friends, and neighbours in return for a "bob", popular name for a shilling. This was to raise much needed funds for the pack or scout group and an element of competition was encouraged to spur everyone on. In reality we would often roam the streets knocking on strangers' doors to tout for jobs, something that would be strongly discouraged in these times of enhanced health and safety. But knock we did, and any house was fair game as long as it did not display the "Job Done" yellow sticker with a big tick. The biggest highlight of the year however was the summer camp which we looked forward to and prepared for all year. This was usually a two-night camp at Tawd Vale Campsite which is still going strong but is now termed an "Adventure Centre". We thought it was a very distant location but in truth was only a short distance away near Ormskirk. We travelled there in the back of a furniture van which a local company, Gilbert Norris, kindly provided. It had no seats of course and despite Akela's stern warning to sit on the floor and keep still, before she made her way to a seat in the driver's cabin, this was impossible to observe and after turning the first corner we were all happily rolling around the floor of the van having great fun. Surprisingly we arrived at the camp with only minor injuries and were all set to have a glorious weekend. The first task was to pitch the tents borrowed from the scouts. They always smelled musty and provided minimum protection from the elements, but we didn't care. We would prepare campfires and later cook sausages and beans for tea. We would go on moonlight walks and during the day there were tracking exercises and all sorts of games. Before bed we would have sing songs around the campfire and later when we were supposed to be asleep we would talk and tell ghost stories until long into the night, tucked snugly in our sleeping bags. It was a splendid time in an environment very different to our usual back drop of terraced streets. I really enjoyed my time as a wolf cub and looked forward to joining the scouts, but we were soon to move house to Netherton, and I never did join the scouts.

Chapter Twelve Days Out and Holidays

"Goodnight campers see you in the morning"

Not all families had an annual holiday in those days, and we did not have a residential holiday every year but if that was the case our Dad would do his best to take us on days out during his summer leave period. A problem was that he was on an annual leave rota, and this did not always coincide with the school holidays. We had some splendid trips out. When we were younger, we could all squeeze onto or into his motorbike and side car and off we would roar. The Welsh coast was always a favourite destination with a day spent in Rhyl which had a lovely beach and funfair. Blackpool was another popular trip particularly when the illuminations were on when we would ride down the promenade with my sister and I standing up in the sidecar with the canvas roof pulled back marvelling at the lights. Chester Zoo was always enjoyable, and I remember being particularly impressed with the pure white, massive polar bears. At other times we would spend the day in Southport or New Brighton in the splendid open-air baths with their diving boards set impossibly high in the air. The water was always freezing but we didn't seem to notice. New Brighton was a very popular destination for day trippers and indeed people staying for their annual week or fortnight holiday. We would get the bus to the Pier Head and then join the crowds of people queuing to board the ferry that took you across the water to New Brighton. You descended down a sloping covered walkway with a huge, curved roof to the floating landing stage, the incline of the walkway depending on the tide. As the ferry docked the deck hands would drop the gangway with an enormous clatter. In good weather people would rush to sit on the outside deck with its long varnished wooden seats ringed with rope and handles as they were designed to serve as life rafts in the event of the boat sinking. There then followed a very pleasing cruise with panoramic views of the waterfront and the docks and up the river to New Brighton. My Dad always joked that you could see our street as you sailed past Bootle but there was a very good view of our church St. James. In those days New Brighton boasted a very impressive pier and the ferry docked at a landing stage adjacent to it. The iron pier was 550 feet long, 70 feet wide and housed a pavilion and other attractions. In later years the ferry service to New Brighton was suspended and sadly the pier was closed and eventually dismantled in 1978. New Brighton had a wonderful beach with lots of rock pools to explore around Fort Perch Rock, a Napoleonic fort built to protect the Mersey during the French Wars. Perch Rock also housed a wonderful lighthouse which was in active use until 1973 although, now in private ownership, it has been restored and a light has been installed which replicates the old signature of two white flashes followed by a red flash (this is only visible from the land). Just across the road from the beach was the funfair which had lots of exciting rides like the Figure 8 roller coaster, the Caterpillar, an enormous Big Wheel and a cable car. It also had a Tower Building which included a ballroom and had been crowned with an actual tower, similar to Blackpool's, until 1896 when it was dismantled. The tower when erected had been the tallest structure in

Britain. The Beatles performed 27 times at the ballroom there, more than at any other venue other than the Cavern, and Little Richard and the Rolling Stones also played there. All in all the resort was a great place for a day out and thousands of people have very fond memories of the place. In fact it was the location for a day out with my very first girlfriend when I was a young teenager. Sadly, New Brighton declined in popularity in the later 1960s but recently it has seen some investment and it is a pleasant place to walk and enjoy the fresh air and views.

Dad took my sister and I on a magical day out which also necessitated a bus journey to the Pier Head one Sunday. This time it was for a cruise on the "Royal Iris", one of the iconic ferries and cruise ships on the River Mersey. Arriving in 1951 she was in continuous service until 1991 and was a well-loved part of the Liverpool scene. She was very distinctive, originally painted in the green and cream colours of the Wallasey Corporation and was fitted out in some luxury with a dance floor and stage, tearoom, cocktail bar and even a fish and chip restaurant. This last facility was the reason why she was commonly known as the "fish and chip boat". In the early 60s Ray McFall the owner of the Cavern Club organised a series of concert cruises, labelled as the "River Boat Shuffles", which sailed out at 07:45 pm and returned at 11:00 pm. These party cruises were very popular at the time and featured some excellent acts. The Beatles appeared a number of times, at first having second billing to Acker Bilk and Johnny Kidd and the Pirates, but later having the top spot. Similar cruises continued later into the 60s and they could be quite rowdy affairs with plenty of beer and alcohol consumed as the boat cruised up and down the river. In the summer Sunday afternoon cruises were very popular with up to 1,000 passengers enjoying the sea air and views as the boat cruised up the river into the Irish Sea. It was one such cruise that my Dad took my sister and I on. When we arrived at the landing stage, we were faced with a huge queue of people lined up and boarding the boat. My Dad drew puzzled looks from some people as he was carrying a small wooden crate of brown ale bottles and, of course, passengers were not allowed to take their own drink on board. Undaunted my Dad stood on the dock and waved up at the crew members on the bridge. The next second the Captain appeared waved to my Dad and spoke to a crew member. Shortly after that the crew member appeared at the top of the gang plank, held up the queue of people boarding and then escorted my Dad, sister and I up on to the ship. We felt like royalty as we walked past all the people waiting to board and once again drew some very puzzled looks. Very soon we were on the bridge and the Captain was greeting my Dad like an old friend which was, of course, exactly what he was. Dad had worked on the docks since leaving the merchant navy in the late 30s and he knew everyone maritime. The Captain and bridge crew made a great fuss of my sister and me and not long after as we sailed up the river the Captain put his hat on my head, stood me on the small crate my Dad had carried aboard which he placed in front of the wheel and then told me that I was in charge of the ship. There I was, hands grasping the wheel, and peering out of the bridge windshield nervously asking the Captain which way to go. "Oh, just keep in the middle of the river and go that way," he replied casually pointing out to sea as he and my Dad sat and nattered and sipped from the bottles of brown ale. I wonder now how the passengers would have reacted to learn that, for some time, their fate lay in the hands of a small boy whose only previous nautical experience consisted of steering a motorboat on Southport boating lake! What the present Health and Safety Executive would make of it is anyone's guess. Later the Captain sent out for fish and chips and lemonade for me and my sister. All in all, it was a magical day, and it is a sad thought that that lovely boat, such an important part of Liverpool's social history, is now rotting away on the southern banks of the Thames just east of the Flood Barrier.

A favourite treat for me during holidays or at the weekend was to spend the day with my Dad when he was on duty down on the docks. This was Gladstone

Dock which at that time was the northern- most dock on the Mersey. My Dad, after a number of years in the merchant marine, became a dock gateman. He was promoted to Pier Master and eventually became Dock Master. I was very proud of him, and he looked very smart in the Mersey Docks and Harbour Board uniform. In 1942 he saw a man floundering in the river and without a second thought stripped off his jacket and jumped from the dock wall into the choppy waters of the Mersey. He was always a strong swimmer and he managed to keep the man afloat until his colleagues threw a life belt into the water which he grasped and managed to swim with the man to a ladder set into the dock wall. He was awarded the Liverpool Shipwreck Humane Society Medal which he made very little of and neglected to have the medal's ribbon sewn onto his uniform. When asked about it he used to joke and say that he spent longer in hospital than the man he rescued and that if he knew the man was a Liverpool supporter, he would have thrown him back in! It was never very clear to me how the man ended up in the river. My Dad was a larger-than-life character and was well known to everyone connected to the docks and he was respected by the men he was in charge of. There was a small hut on the dock provided for the gatemen with a small fire, stove, table and chairs and a bunk. It was very cosy. Dad used to make me butties of "connyonny" (condensed milk) or jam or lemon curd and tea with "connyonny" milk in place of milk and sugar. Dad worked shifts of 7am to 3pm, 3pm to 11pm and nights of 11pm to 7am. Most times I would accompany him on the 3 to 11 shift. It was a fascinating place for a young boy to spend time. The other workers made a great fuss of me, and ships would arrive from exotic places around the world. Language differences were never a problem for Dad as he issued instructions to the foreign crews as he always maintained that you just had to shout a bit louder to be understood – in defiance of logic this seemed to work. He particularly welcomed ships from Spanish speaking countries as according to him you just had to add an "O" or "A" on the end of an English word to convert it into Spanish. I particularly liked the evenings when the red and green dock lights came on and arriving ships were ablaze with light. If I became a little sleepy, I could always have a little nap in the bunk which was hugely comfortable. On occasion the skipper of the pilot boat would take me out on the river as we sailed out to the Irish Sea to allow the pilot to board an arriving vessel and at other times, I would board a dredger. Dredging the river to keep the shipping lanes clear was a constant task and the boats would suck up huge amounts of silt to dump in the Irish Sea. They also sucked up different species of fish which I was really interested in having an interest in angling. Small sharks, rays and huge eels could sometimes be spotted together with a whole variety of fish and crustaceans. It was a source of great disappointment to me that when I fished off the dock wall, which I occasionally did, I never managed to catch any of the fish I saw in the dredgers, and I had to be content with a few small flatties if I was lucky.

Dad was always supportive of my hobbies and encouraged me when I became interested in fishing. I was switched on to this by following the adventures of Mr. Crabtree, a character created by Bernard Venables in the Daily Mirror newspaper. It was a cartoon series that was eventually published in a book "Mr. Crabtree Goes Fishing" in which he and son Peter set about on fishing trips throughout the fishing year. Mr. Crabtree seemed very posh to me as he wore a suit and tie for fishing and had a large study in his house to store all his fishing tackle. He made fishing seem very straight forward and he never failed to catch lots of huge fish while smoking a large pipe. Unfortunately, I found the reality very different and to me fishing was a lot more difficult and frustrating and presented far more challenges than it seemed to offer Peter and his fishing genius Dad. Sadly, my original copy of the paper bound book had long disintegrated, but I was delighted when the book was reprinted a few years ago to mark the 50th. anniversary of its first publication. I still enjoy leafing through the book and its beautiful illustrations although the equipment and techniques used look very dated now. My first set of tackle was a small fibre glass rod and fixed spool reel which I used for the first time during a Butlin's holiday. I set up by the camp's shallow boating lake much to the amusement of other campers, who assured me that I was wasting my time as there were no fish in it, but to my astonishment, using only small flakes of bread, I proceeded to catch over 50 roach in short order. I attracted a small audience, equally as surprised as I and although the fish were only small I silently thanked Mr. Crabtree and judged myself to be a worthy student of his. Unfortunately, in the years that followed and judging by my angling success, beginner's luck just about covers it. The thought often occurred to me during the long fruitless days of fishless fishing trips that the problem was that, although I was doing everything right following the guidance in Mr. Crabtree's book, clearly the fish had not read the book themselves! Even so I had some lovely days out with my Dad when we would set out on his motorbike to our local canal the Leeds to Liverpool, the Shropshire Union Canal, Carr Mill Dam near St. Helens or some other lake or river.

Days out were great, but they could not compare with a week's holiday away from home. We did not go away every year, but we had some memorable holidays, and this was at a time when not every family could afford a stay away from home. One of my earliest memories of holidaying was when we all packed into my Dad's motorbike and sidecar and roared off to a chalet on the coast near Gronant, North Wales. I say a chalet but when I looked at a photograph taken outside the chalet, which I came across recently, the building looks more like a large, rather run-down garden shed. Even so we had a fine time playing on the beach and paddling in the sea.

My Mum, sister and I outside our luxury bungalow!

A few years later we had a very enjoyable holiday in the Isle of Man. This involved the family and our suitcases packing into a black hackney cab for the journey to the Pier Head. This was my very first trip in a taxi and it was very exciting. I felt very sophisticated waving to my friends in the street who

143

had gathered to see us off, a taxi not being a common sight in our street. At the Pier Head we boarded the Isle of Man Steam Packet boat the "Manxman". This appeared huge in my eyes with its black and white livery and red and black funnel, and it was twice as big as the "Royal Iris". The ship was cast in the role of RMS "Carpathia", the first ship to recue survivors and, incidentally, which my maternal grandfather claimed to be serving on, for the 1979 dramatic film "S.O.S Titanic". We were going on holiday with my mother's sister and family, and we all crowded into one of the very comfortable lounges on the ship. The sailing took four hours and it was very exciting to sail up the river and out into the Irish Sea. Our excitement did not last for long as the seas became increasingly rough. We all felt sick and miserable except for Dad who had retained his sea legs from his time in the merchant marine. He made things worse by tucking into an enormous bacon butty as he stood and swayed with the roll of the tide. He was scornful of our complaints about the rough sea. "You call this rough," he cheerfully observed and then proceeded to terrify us with tales of terrible storms, huge seas and disastrous shipwrecks. He was having a fine time. Eventually we neared the island, and the seas began to abate as we headed for the port of Douglas. It was a beautiful sight as we sailed into the harbour with the pretty town of Douglas laid out before us surrounded by a range of beautiful hills. Best of all was that as we stepped ashore the sun was shining and the seagulls were wheeling about. "Oh, this is lovely!" my older cousin exclaimed as she breathed in the salt tang of the sea air just as a huge seagull delivered a sloppy welcome all over her new and pretty summer frock. She was horrified and not at all comforted by my Dad's assurance that this was a sign of good luck. We walked to our boarding house which was not far from the sea front, and we thought it was very grand. The bedrooms were large with carpet on the floor and, although the rooms were not en-suite, we did have a bathroom and inside toilet which was a luxury for us. We had a proper cooked breakfast each morning and a three-course evening meal, so we were very happy. The Isle of Man seemed very exotic to our eyes, and we were very lucky with the weather which remained fine and dry all week and there were a lot of things to do. I was intrigued by the fact that Manx cats did not have tails and I always checked this out when I spotted a cat. Equally puzzling was the Manx flag with its three legs on a red background – what could it mean? Douglas was a lovely town with its harbour, sea front promenade, which was strung with pretty lights at night and a beach with plenty of golden sand, interesting rock pools for us to explore and donkey rides. We enjoyed riding on the horse drawn tram way (the oldest surviving in Britain) which took us to Victoria Pier in the red carriages pulled by the enormous shire horses. For a longer journey we took the Isle of Man Railway, a steam operated narrow gauge railway, to Port Erin a pretty seaside village in the south-west of the island. On another day we travelled on the Manx Electric railway to Laxey, a very scenic journey, to visit the famous Laxey Wheel built into the hillside above the village. It was an impressive sight which is not surprising as it is the largest working water wheel in the world. We had a great time in the Isle of Man and were very sorry when the week came to an end, and we boarded the boat back to Liverpool – but at least the sea was calm on the return journey.

Nowadays a trip to Disneyland in Florida is generally regarded as the dream family holiday. This would have been beyond our comprehension back in the 1960s as the idea of travelling to America would have been an impossible thought. The only people we knew who had actually been to the USA were merchant seamen like my Dad. The popular dream holiday in our day was a trip to Butlin's and even this was beyond the budget of most families in our street. However, one Christmas my Dad made the dramatic announcement that the following summer he had booked a week's holiday in the Butlin's camp in Pwllheli in North Wales. My sister and I could not contain our excitement even though August seemed a long way in the future. We could not wait to brag about our news to our friends in the street. Despite the long wait the much-anticipated day drew near. Families could not afford the extensive holiday wardrobes which is the expectation now but even, so we had been on several shopping trips to kit ourselves out in summer clothing for the holiday. This did not extend beyond a few T shirts, shorts, a pair of sandals and one swimming costume. A couple of days before the great day I was dragged to the barbers for a short back and sides and the night before Dad and I walked to the public baths in Marsh Lane for a steaming soak. It was certainly a change from the tin bath in the back kitchen and I was amazed at the size of the tub which was easily big enough and deep enough for me to swim in. A sleepless night followed, and I waited anxiously for the hackney cab to arrive in the morning to whisk us off to the Ribble bus station in Skelhorne Street in Liverpool to board the coach bound for Butlin's. The atmosphere on the coach was electric, packed with families and children just as wound up as my sister and me. We all felt like celebrities as the coach pulled out of the indoor station waved off by other family members and friends. The journey took almost four hours, but this included a lengthy stop near Bodelwyddan on the A55 where there was a café and several shops. I remember gazing up at Bodelwyddan Castle and thinking what a wonderful place it would be to visit. After food, drink, and a visit to the toilet we were on our way driving past the beautiful gothic marble church of St. Margaret of Antioch with its huge spire. Not long after we would drive through the tunnel where the driver would beep his horn, a tradition which continues to this day. We were told this was to pay respect to the fairies. Every child tried to be the first to spot the flags which marked the entrance to the camp, and we could hardly contain ourselves as the coach drove through the gated and guarded entrance. The first task after retrieving our cases was to join the organised chaos in the huge reception hall. Eventually we would reach one of the receptionists and receive the keys to our chalets, location maps and the daily entertainments guide. Butlin's camps were divided into houses, Windsor, Gloucester, Kent and Warwick. Houses were colour coded and during the week numerous competitions were contested between the houses with house points to be earned. Campers were strongly encouraged to take part and their competitive enthusiasm was whipped up by the Redcoats who would cajole the most reluctant to join in and would rarely take no for an answer. At the end of the week the winning house would be announced with great fanfare. We were always keen to learn which house we were in and then would do all we could to earn points and persuade our parents and older relatives to get involved. We always persuaded our Dad to enter the famous Knobbly Knees competition, although it did not take much effort as he was always up for a laugh and joke. To my Mum's embarrassment he would parade around the ballroom with the other contestants all with their trousers rolled up to display their knees to the judging panel. To our great joy, at least that of the younger members of our party, one year he actually won and for the rest of the week proudly wore his winner's medal. We had several Butlin's holidays always together with various aunts, uncles, and cousins. After reception we had to find our chalets, which was not an easy task. You could queue for a minibus or a miniature train to take you to a drop off point near your chalet, but we were always keen to unload the cases and begin our holiday as soon as possible so we would trudge off carrying the cases and armed with the camp map. The chalets were arranged in four areas based on the houses and there were a bewildering number of them, all laid out in rows with grass lawns and flower beds separating them. After many false starts we would eventually find our allocated chalets. Judged by today's standards they were pretty basic. Most were in single storey rows but there were some two-storey blocks. The chalets were small, with small beds, a wardrobe, a sink, and a bedside cupboard. They were unheated with a tiled floor and had stippled walls which could be quite uncomfortable if you moved against them in your sleep. Each row had a large toilet block with several bathtubs. The small windows had vivid coloured curtains with a yacht design which did little to keep out the light. We thought it was all wonderful even if we planned to spend as little time in the chalets as possible as the camp had such a wealth of facilities and entertainments to keep us constantly occupied. The camp was like a mini town with shops, hairdressers, newsagents and post office but of more interest to us, indoor and outdoor swimming pools, sports ground, a fairground, theatres, dancehall with live groups, theatre, boating lake, chairlift to take you to the beautiful beach, a miniature railway and even a small zoo. We felt as if we were in heaven and best of all it was all free. For most of the day we kids were allowed to roam free taking full advantage of everything on offer and we touched base with our parents at the three mealtimes and then later in the evening in a bar lounge or the dancehall when we could listen to the live group, bob about on the dance floor and if we were lucky wash down a hotdog with a bottle of Pepsi Cola just like in the American movies. Our days were jam packed with activities. We were woken in the morning by a ringing tone blasted out by the speaker in our chalet. If this didn't wake you then the song that followed would – "Zippy Do Do Dah, Zippy Do Day", is impossible to sleep through. Not that we needed much persuasion as we were keen to seize the day. The Redcoat speaking on the tannoy would invite us to breakfast which was served in our house dining room, a huge room with row upon row of tables. Our party was allocated a couple of tables for the week and breakfast, lunch and dinner were served there. All meals were served by the team of young waiters and waitresses who did a great job in serving the hundreds of campers in no time at all. There was virtually no choice, but we thought the food was wonderful. A full English breakfast with toast and jam was a welcome change to our usual porridge and this was washed down with tea, coffee or juice and milk for us kids. Lunch was a three-course feast with soup, a main of meat or fish, potatoes and vegetables and a pudding and evening dinner was very similar. In the evening the Redcoats would spin a large wheel and if the arrow settled on your table number you won a bottle of "Champagne", (in reality a bottle of fizzy wine). This was presented by a parade of Redcoats with great fanfare and thunderous applause from the campers. To our great disappointment our table number never came up. Another feature of mealtimes was the huge cheer that went up when one of the serving staff, working at great speed, dropped and smashed a plate. To our joy this happened quite often. We really enjoyed mealtimes, but we kids bolted it down as fast as we could because there was so much to do and we were keen to be out and about. There was a huge outdoor swimming pool with diving boards that were scarily high even to jump off and a very elaborate fountain feature that you could clamber on. We did brave the outdoor pool but given the unreliable British weather the indoor pool was a safer and warmer bet. Compared to Balliol Road Baths the indoor pool was exciting and exotic. It was large with plenty of space surrounding it with benches. The glass ceiling let in lots of light and hanging from it were tropical plants and flowers which gave it a Caribbean feel but most impressive was the fact that it boasted glass panels set underwater. Wearing goggles, we could dive down and wave to the adults in our party sitting in the lounge below having a drink. When we had had enough swimming, we could take a rowboat on the very scenic boating lake. One of my cousins would sit in the bow and push the front of the boat up and down to create large waves which would threaten to capsize other boats. Alternatively, we would turn pirate and try to ram the boats crewed by other children. We would continue creating mayhem until the boat keepers called us in or threatened to ban us from the boating lake altogether! From there we would often make for the chair lifts which took you on a long ride, high above the fields, to the beach. It was a very pleasant and peaceful trip until, safely out of sight of the ride attendants, one of our party would begin to rock the cable car making it sway perilously accompanied by the screams of my younger cousins.

On the chair lift with my sister and cousin

The beach was beautiful and the sea very inviting although often too cold for bathing. There were lots of rock pools to explore and plenty of space on the sands to play. After lunch we usually visited the fair for the afternoon session. There were many exciting rides like the Waltzer, Speedway, Big Wheel and Bumping Cars but my favourite was the Trabant a large disc with carriages which spun you around, tilted at a very steep angle and then repeated the whole thing backwards. It was great fun, and we would run from one ride to another to try and cram in as many rides as possible. We were always hungry and very ready for our evening meal and after that we would accompany our parents to a show in the Gaiety

Theatre. The productions were a mix of professional entertainers and Redcoats often with game shows with willing campers taking part. Later we would make our way to the ballroom which featured a live group. Many famous entertainers began their careers at Butlin's camps. Des O'Connor was a Redcoat at Ayr as was Jimmy Tarbuck at Pwllheli, Cliff Richard at Clacton-on-Sea and other famous entertainers who began at Butlin's include Dave Allen, Terry Scott, and Ted Rogers. Famously Ringo Starr was a drummer in the band Rory Storm and the Hurricanes who played a three-month residency at Pwllheli in 1960. In 1962 Ringo was performing with the band in the Skegness camp when he was visited by John Lennon and Paul McCartney to discuss the possibility of Ringo joining the Beatles. In a phone call a few weeks later Ringo accepted John's offer to join the band. The rest, as they say, is history. It is very possible that I met some entertainers who would later become stars and may well have had their autograph as we collected them in our little books, but if I did, I am unaware of it and my autograph book is long gone. Even so we made a very enthusiastic audience and thoroughly enjoyed everything on offer. At some point every evening we would persuade our parents to part with some change, and we would head off to the arcade. We would spend our pennies on the slot machines and roller penny games although my favourite was the horse racing game where you could bet on your horse with a three-penny bit. Needless to say, we would stay until all our money was gone but it was good fun. To finish off our perfect day, if our parents were in an alcohol induced good humour, we would be treated to a hot dog and Pepsi- we felt so sophisticated. This was living life just like in the movies and it could just not get any better. But a week was soon over, and we had to leave our chalet, board the coach and head back to Liverpool. The air of despondency on the coach was palpable as we contemplated a return to school and the streets of Bootle, which seemed so grey and dull after the colour and excitement of Butlin's.

Chapter Thirteen Football

"We're on our way to Wembley we shall not be moved"

When two Scousers meet for the first time a question will inevitably arise at some point, "Red or Blue?" For the vast majority of people living on Merseyside there will be no prevarication or hesitation, even from those who never, or rarely, attend matches. Neutrals are a rarity even among those who do not really care for football. Loyalties are often family based but there are many examples of mixed marriages and families split in their support. Jim, a friend of mine, was a participant in "Who wants to be a millionaire?" and Chris Tarrant noticing that my friend was a Blue, but his wife Jane was a Red, said "There must be some arguments in your house!" Quick as a flash my friend rejoined, "Only on Saturdays." For anyone born and brought up on Merseyside in the 50s and 60s football was a hugely important part of life. Any young boy like me who was not totally useless at kicking a ball had only one ambition and that was to be a professional footballer preferably with the team he supported. Together with many of my friends and schoolmates, if I was not playing or watching football, then I was dreaming about wearing the blue of Everton and the white shirt of England. My Dad was a committed Evertonian, and his dad had supported them from boyhood which reached back into the early history of the club. My Dad, as a teenager, was in the huge crowd that saw Dixie Dean score his record breaking 60th goal in the Football League Division 1. He raised my brother and me on tales of the legendary Dixie, Tommy Lawton, and T.G. Jones, the "Prince of Centre Halves." In fact, for many years he, like many football fans on Merseyside, regularly attended the games of both clubs – Everton one Saturday and Liverpool the next in that time of sensible and predictable fixture lists and games that took place on Saturday afternoons. This practice was recognised for many years when the clubs produced a shared programme. Gradually it fell out of fashion and fans concentrated on their first love and rivalries became more intense even though this manifested itself in a more or less friendly atmosphere. When I was younger you would often witness Blue and Red fans making their way together to derbies and Blues fans would occupy part of the Kop, on the left-hand side, for those games. When both sides dominated English football in the 80s Blues and Reds travelled together for their Merseyside Wembley finals - there was rarely any trouble and the sight of a dad with a red scarf consoling his wife and children wearing blue scarves after a Liverpool victory was a heart-warming sight – but I do so wish it had been the other way around! I cannot remember the first match my Dad took me to but I do know, that like my brother before me, he carried me over the turnstile as a child in his arms after he had paid for his admission. It is very likely that my Dad knew the gatekeeper as he seemed to know everyone. He would make his way to his favourite spot on the Gladys Street terrace just under the stand on the right behind the barrier – incidentally the exact same spot I would occupy years later with my own friends. On the barrier Dad would place a rolled-up mac' as a cushion and that was my seat for the match. His friends would rustle my hair, give me sweets, and make a fuss of me. If Everton won, which they often did, they would say I had brought good luck and give me small gifts of money. Dad often attended reserve games every other Saturday and I remember running up and down the terrace steps when the action on the pitch failed to hold my attention. However, it was magical visiting Goodison

Park with its huge floodlights and towering stands. In those days the ground was regarded as one of the country's finest stadiums and this was confirmed when it was chosen to host games in the 1966 World Cup. Emerging from the steep staircase at the rear of the Gladys Street and seeing the vast expanse of green and the tiered stands surrounding the ground was an impressive sight which never failed to impress and which the black and white television pictures of the time could never hope to replicate. I continued to attend games with my Dad until I became too big to carry over the turnstile. It was then time for me to undergo that seminal rite of passage which faced many young Evertonians in those days and that was to become a member of the famous and notorious Boys' Pen. Many accounts have been written about this famous Everton institution including a very accurate and amusing piece by an ex-colleague of mine which I highly recommend. ("Only the strong survived" by Paul McParlan which can be found on Toffeeweb and in a number of other publications.) It was located at the rear on the left of the Gladys Street. The admission price was half that of the normal terrace admission and it was, in theory, limited to those under 14 years of age. In those days we walked to Goodison together with other people from the street, a distance of about two and a half miles. Dad would join his mates in the pub before the game and I would stand outside with other children clutching a bottle of pop and a bag of crisps. Dad would then escort me safely to the Boys' Pen entrance and after that any notion of safety ended. The Pen was ruled by the older boys who not only bagged the best spots but also the sweets and money of the younger boys who often had to resort to watching the match from the furthest corner of the enclosure with a very restricted view of the pitch. As you got older and attended with a group of mates you gradually ascended the pecking order, becoming safer and securing a much better view of the game. The atmosphere was electric and often the Pen would be chanting and singing, albeit in a distinctive high falsetto when other parts of the ground had become quiet. Enclosing the Pen was a wall of sharp fencing, which at some stage was reinforced with mesh, as it was the ambition of any "Penner" to scale the fence and join the adults in the crowd. A number of times I witnessed intrepid dare devils crawling along the stanchions in the roof of the stands, risking life and limb to achieve their goal. Despite enduring the privations of life in the Pen (I have not referenced the toilets for obvious reasons and the sake of decency) it was worth it to witness what was a golden era for the club. Harry Catterick had assembled a team that would win the title, for the first time since the Second World War, in1963 and the FA Cup in 1966. Players like Alex Young, Roy Vernon and the young Colin Harvey were worshipped by the fans. It is still one of

the great disappointments in my life that I could not
secure a ticket for the 1966 Cup Final. In those days
clubs in the final only received 14,000 tickets and
even season ticket holders, like my Dad and brother,
were fortunate to get one. But they did and I was
reduced to the role of waving them and a couple of
their friends off in my brother's minivan on the
Friday afternoon before the game. They had a
wonderful trip and my brother often spoke about it as
one of his top highlights in many years of supporting
the Blues. Everton, of course, came from two goals
down to win the game and the stadium became a sea
of blue and white delirious Scousers singing their
hearts out. Although watching on our small black and
white television I, like many others, was caught up in
the excitement and after the game ran into the street
to recreate the goals with my friends. At least on the
Sunday I was there in town with thousands of others
to cheer our heroes home and the atmosphere was
electric. How sad to think that now the FA Cup has
lost some of its glamour and the oldest cup
competition in the world is treated with such
disrespect by some of the so-called top teams. The
excitement that summer did not end with Everton's
victory as the World Cup was coming to England for
the first time. My Dad and brother had a book of
tickets for all the games played at Goodison and they
witnessed some fabulous games and great teams like
Brazil, Portugal and Hungary. The Goodison crowed

thrilled to the skills of Pele, Garrincha and Tostao although the Brazilians never really hit their stride losing to Hungary and Portugal. Eusebio the "Black Panther" orchestrated a thrilling 3-1 victory over Brazil and won the affection of the Evertonians by stating that Goodison Park was the best stadium of his playing life. However, this did not count for much in the quarter final when Portugal were to face the competition's surprising unfancied North Koreans who had beaten the mighty Italians in their final group game. Many of the supporters in the crowd followed the Liverpool tradition of cheering on the underdogs and they took the plucky Asians to their hearts. So enamoured was one of my brother's friends with the Koreans that he learnt the team's names by heart and could recite them on demand. Amazingly this support from the crowd had the desired effect as the Koreans stormed into a three nil lead. It was not to last, and Portugal secured victory aided by a hat trick from Eusebio who won the tournament's Golden Boot Award. Many fans on Merseyside felt cheated as England's semi-final against Portugal, scheduled to be played in Liverpool, was moved to Wembley and instead Goodison hosted the West Germany and USSR game. Very few fans from Merseyside secured a ticket for the Wembley final and so had to be content at watching on their black and white televisions. Of course, we were pleased with England's triumph but in truth it could not compare with Everton's FA Cup win or, for the other side of Merseyside, Liverpool's Division One title. There is no doubt that Merseyside was the undisputed capital of English football at that time, and this was made clear at the Charity Shield match held at Goodison in August when before the game both teams performed a lap of honour with the Everton captain Brian Labone holding the FA Cup and Ron Yeats, the Liverpool captain, holding the Division One trophy. Behind them came Roger Hunt of Liverpool and Ray Wilson of Everton holding the small but beautiful, golden, Jules Rimet World Cup. I stood on the Bullen's Road terrace as close to the pitch as I could, and it was a glorious sight to see those famous trophies glinting in the sunshine – there really was no finer place for any football fan to be and it is a sight that will never be repeated. Unfortunately, Liverpool won the game with a goal from "Sir Roger Hunt" but we Evertonians know how to swallow our disappointments. Revenge was not long in coming. Shortly after this game Everton signed arguably the finest player in the England squad as Alan Ball left Blackpool for Goodison Park. He was an instant success and just two weeks later we were roaring our delight as he scored two goals in a 3-1 victory at home against Liverpool. "Ball of Fire" and "Having a Ball" screamed the newspapers' sport's headlines, and we had a new hero to worship. With his red hair, iconic white boots and non-stop running Alan Ball became a legend in the club's history. The following March he played a pivotal role in one of the most memorable encounters between the Merseyside rivals. This was at a time when the nation would come to a halt at one o' clock on the Monday after FA Cup rounds which had all been played on Saturday at three o' clock. We gathered around radios, at school in my case, to listen as the next draw was made during a meeting of the Board of the Football Association. We waited to hear our team's number as the balls were placed in a bag, shaken, and then drawn out one by one. To our relief Everton were drawn at home and then, to our great excitement, the number for Liverpool was drawn. Another Merseyside Derby with a quarter final place for the winners! Rivalry between the teams was arguably at its peak and there was great anticipation on Merseyside looking forward to the match and, of course, defeat was unthinkable. Demand for tickets was such that a decision was made to hold the game at 7:00 pm to enable the match to be shown at Anfield on large screens. Over 100,000 watched the match live, 65,000 at Goodison and 40,000 at Anfield. I was fortunate to be at Goodison and watched the game with my Dad and brother from the Park End Stand – I'm not sure why as both my Dad and brother had season tickets for Bullen's Road. The build up to the game was tremendous and I am not sure I will ever experience an atmosphere quite like it again. As I walked down the steps to take my seat it was almost like there was electricity in the air and I could actually feel the hair on my head begin to stand up. The roar as the teams walked out of the tunnel could be heard for miles. The Everton fans sang their favourite songs at the top of their lungs, "Oh we hate Bill Shankly, and we hate St. John," and "We shall not be moved," and to be fair the smaller Red contingent competed well with "You'll Never Walk Alone" and others from their repertoire and before we knew it the game was underway. In truth, like many Derbies, it was not a great game of football – there was too much tension and too much at stake at for players to play their normal game – but just before half time came the defining moment of the game when Alan Ball, seizing on a poor back pass, swivelled just outside the six-yard box and fired a glorious effort into the net. What joy! The ground erupted and if I did not love Alan Ball before this I did now. During the second half Everton defended stoutly despite fierce Liverpool attacks and I do not think any Blue fan finished the match with finger nails but at last the final whistle blew followed by rapturous celebrations amongst the Blue fans. I floated home that evening on a cloud of euphoria with dreams of Wembley filling my head. Sadly, it lasted only a few weeks and came to an abrupt end as I stood on the terraces of the City Ground as Everton lost to Nottingham Forest in the most disappointing fashion in the sixth round. Oh well such is the life of an Evertonian! However, I did not have to wait too long to make up for the disappointment of missing out on the 1966 Wembley trip. In 1968 I attended all Everton home games and every game of the FA cup run. I now watched the games from the Gladys Street terrace standing in the same spot my Dad had vacated as he and my brother now had season tickets in the Bullen's Road stand. After away ties at Southport and Carlisle Everton overcame Tranmere Rovers at home and then defeated Leicester at Filbert Street to set up a semi-final against Leeds at Old Trafford. A penalty scored by Johnny Morrissey clinched Everton's place at Wembley. This time I secured my ticket as I was a season ticket holder and I even managed to get a ticket for my cousin through the vouchers issued with the home programmes. So it was that on Friday 17th. May my Dad, my cousin and I set off for London. We drove down in my Dad's Reliant Robin which he purchased after discovering that it could be driven on a motorcycle license, as he preferred not to go through the ordeal of lessons and a driving test. Looking for all the world like Dell Boy and friends on a Jolly Boys' outing we cruised down the M6 and M1 with blue scarves flying from the windows and sounding the horn every few minutes as we spotted other members of the Blue Army. My Dad was nothing if not a creature of habit and we followed the exact same plan he had followed in 1966. He had booked two nights in a boarding house in Watford and from there it was a short 25 minute rail journey into London. The boarding house was close to Watford's ground and to my young eyes looked a little forbidding being a large, old, Victorian terrace. Dad greeted the owner, who looked and sounded just like Alf Garnett in "Till Death Us Do Part", like a long-lost buddy. We arrived in the early evening and Dad whisked us off to London on the train to see some of the sights and to have a meal. It was all very exciting as this was my first visit to the capital and eating out was a rare treat. My cousin and I were suitably impressed with the lights of Piccadilly Circus and Leicester Square, and it was not long before Dad pointed to a restaurant and said, "This will do." It was an Italian restaurant, dimly lit with candles and full of couples having a romantic night out. We attracted a good deal of attention decked out as we were in blue and white scarves, plastic sombreros, that were all the rage for that final and rosettes. The waiter, who was looking us up and down rather dubiously, seated us at a table near the window which soon became apparent, was a mistake. We peered at the menu in some confusion never having eaten Italian before and not having a clue what the dishes were or what to order. We need not have worried. After a few minutes groups of fellow Blues began to drift past the window and when they spotted us, resplendent in our club colours, they hammered on the window –

"EVERTON, EVERTON." Of course, we were obligated to respond, and this did not lend itself to the quiet, romantic ambience in the restaurant. The waiter came over and quietly insisted that we leave. We did not argue and in truth it was something of a relief as we felt so out of place. We were far happier with hotdogs from a street vendor who did not mind in the least our joining in with the chanting of fellow Scousers. That night I hardly slept as visions of my team parading around Wembley with the cup kept me awake. Dad had us up early the next day and after an enormous English breakfast cooked by Alf's wife, who disappointingly did not look at all like Dandy Nichols, we were back on the train to London. Dad was determined to show us as many of the sites as possible before the game and we made good use of the Tube. We gazed at Buckingham Palace as we walked up the Mall, marvelled at Big Ben, the Houses of Parliament and Tower Bridge. In those more innocent times, we were able to stroll up Downing Street and stand outside number 10. It was not until 1989 that the street was closed to the public. A lone policeman guarded the entrance, and he was very kind and friendly and allowed us to stand on the step. I so wish we had thought to bring a camera. The Prime Minister was Harold Wilson who was MP for Huyton and of course, a great favourite of my Dad's being Labour. What a thrill it would have been if he had come walking out of the door! Despite the splendour of the London sights, we were itching to get to Wembley and were soon on our way. As impressive as the new stadium is I do not think it can compare with the beauty and grandeur of the original stadium – despite its inadequate toilet facilities! I will never forget my first view of the historic stadium as we walked up Empire Way. The sheer size of the place with its signature twin towers was a breath-taking site. Dad keen to wet his whistle took us to a table outside the Torch pub near the stadium. As we sat there crowds of Everton fans drifted past, and I was amazed how many of them recognised my Dad – he seemed to know everyone and there was much hand shaking and back slapping before we eventually made our way to the teams' entrance gates to cheer the boys in blue as they arrived by coach. As we walked to our entrance there was a commotion as a group of fans crowded around Paul McCartney as he walked to the stadium. I am not sure how keen an Evertonian he was as I do not think any of the Beatles were particularly interested in football. Certainly, in later years when the club was desperate for finance McCartney showed no desire to invest in Everton. In those days most of the ground was standing terraces and we stood behind one of the goals with thousands of other Evertonians. A huge elliptical roof covered all the stands and terraces, and this helped to generate the deafening noise as both sets of supporters sang their favourite songs and roared out their chants. The atmosphere was electric, and the noise drowned out the military band which was the pre-match entertainment in those days. A man in a white suit climbed a rostrum to lead the traditional community singing but we the fans preferred our own songs until we reached the time for the Wembley Hymn "Abide with me" which both sets of supporters belted out with much more enthusiasm than they did for the National Anthem. Soon it was time for the teams to walk up the tunnel to a deafening ovation. Everton were in their change strip of amber and blue and I was proud to wave my amber and blue scarf knitted specially for the final by my auntie. The teams lined up to be introduced to the Guest of Honour the Princess Alexandra who was surprised to be roundly booed by the Everton half of the ground. Nothing personal here but perhaps someone should have advised her that Evertonians would not look favourably on her wearing a coat in the colours of Liverpool FC. We Blues were confident of victory particularly as we had beaten West Brom 6-2 in a recent league game but sadly it was not to be. After dominating the game and producing numerous chances we failed to score and in extra time Jeff Astle broke our hearts. I do not think I have ever been more disappointed before or since and I could sympathise with Alan Ball who threw his loser's medal on the pitch in disgust. There would be no dancing in the fountains that night and we made our dejected way back to Watford where Alf Garnett was full of sympathy and to console my Dad took him off to the Watford supporters' club to drown his sorrows. This left my cousin and I to sit in the boarding house eating a fish and chips supper and reliving our misery by watching the game's highlights on Match of the Day, in black and white even though this was the first final to be televised in colour. The next day we made our weary way back to Merseyside full of sadness, but we would have been happier if we had known that we were to see some of the finest football played by our club the following season and the season after that romp home as League Champions. However, it would not be until 1984 that I would witness Everton winning the FA Cup.

Chapter Fourteen Moving to Netherton

"We need you up in Dodge City, son, cause there's so many bad guys"

In his excellent book "The Lost Tribe of Everton and Scottie Road" Ken Rogers describes life in those very close-knit working-class communities and how neighbours, family and friends were dispersed to a very different environment in distant new towns in Kirby, Speke and Skelmersdale and something very valuable was lost in the process. Literally, life was never the same again for many who found themselves re-housed, some in high rise monstrosities and living a great distance from everything they knew and were familiar with. By contrast Bootle's slum clearance scheme took a different approach. The "Welsh" streets community off Marsh Lane and other parts of the town were re-housed in new council estates not too far away and residents could choose, to some extent, the house or flat they desired. This resulted in the new areas retaining something of the old community spirit with friends and families managing to live close to one another. It was a short distance up the road to Netherton which was a part of Bootle. The houses were well built with inside bathrooms and gardens and although the area had its own shops on Park Lane and the Marian Square, it was only a short ride on the 28 bus back to the shops on Strand Road. My mother's family had all moved together and had houses close to one another on the Park Lane estate where all the roads were named after cathedrals, and which existed in the shadow of the huge English Electric works. In 1964 my parents had the opportunity to move to Netherton by means of a house exchange with another family. I think they felt that with my Mum's continuing ill health it would benefit her to be closer to her sisters and so early in that year Gilbert Norris loaded our possessions into one of their vans and we waved goodbye to our friends and neighbours before embarking on the short journey to Chester Avenue. Our house was in a close

172

with flats situated in the corners and houses in between. Compared to our Bootle house this new house was well built and we now had an inside bathroom and toilet and so from now on did not need our wellies to spend a penny on cold winter nights. The house had a small entrance hall, a large living/dining room, a kitchen with hot and cold water and a small storage room which we called the outhouse which had a small cupboard for storing the smokeless fuel for the fire. The fire was situated in the living room and was an integrated unit with a glass door designed to burn smokeless fuel. It generated a lot of heat and also heated water but the best thing about it was that it could be dampened down overnight to be restarted the next day. It even had a gas poker to aid ignition – no more perilous attempts to start the fire with a shovel and newspaper. The house did not have central heating, but Dad placed a couple of electric free-standing heaters to warm the bedrooms and the bathroom had an electric wall heater so we were pretty cosy. A front garden and a decent sized back garden were very welcome and all in all we were very pleased with our new home. My Mum's three sisters and her niece lived very close and so I was never far away from my cousins and as my parents knew many neighbours, most of whom came from the Marsh Lane area, we felt very much at home. However, as a new kid on the block, it did take time for me to find my place in the pecking order and given my attitude of not backing down and the fact that there were some real hard cases on the estate, I finished runner up in a number of scraps. On one occasion I was doing particularly badly against another boy when my sister, who was always looking out for me and afraid of no one, came rushing to my rescue and whacked my opponent on the back with the brush pole. He later said it almost killed him and of course in time, mainly through our shared interest in football, we became friends. To show there was no hard feelings my sister became his brother's girlfriend and later his wife. What really forged my place on the estate was the fact that I was not completely useless at football, and I eventually summoned up the courage to take part in the Sunday football game that took place on the local school field. Most of the boys from the estate participated and ranged in age from twelve-year-olds like me to young adults. The game kicked off after lunch and lasted all afternoon. Some of the older boys would come directly from an early liquid lunch at the Park Hotel, or "Nark" Hotel as it was often accurately referred to, and the games were lively to say the least with no quarter given or asked for. Some of the tackling was closer to grievous bodily harm and sometimes so late that the perpetrators, often those who had been imbibing the barley at lunchtime, could only have imagined that they were still playing in last week's game. There was no referee and decisions always went in favour of the most aggressive with little regard for the actual laws of the game. It was a very daunting experience for a young boy like me but after a while I learnt to hold my own and was awarded something approaching a grudging respect from the older boys and hard cases. I steadily made my way up the pecking order and eventually I was one of the first to be picked instead of one of the last. As I made my way around the estate, often referred to as "Dodge", a reference to the lawless Wild West Dodge City, I would receive a nod of recognition from even the toughest boys who regarded the estate as their own territory. Years later when meeting up for an annual reunion meal with my old school friends I would share a taxi with one of them. Delta taxis are famous in Liverpool and their drivers are often interesting characters to say the least. It became a standing joke that for four years on the run I knew the taxi driver in each case as they were acquaintances from back in the day on the estate. My friend John asked sarcastically if I knew every Delta driver. Come the fifth year we get into the taxi and to my friend's smug satisfaction I did not recognise the driver but when I asked for a drop off at my sister's, who still lived in Chester Avenue, the driver said "Dodge?" and looked at me in the mirror. "Brian how are you doing?" he asked. Sure enough it was another of the players who had kicked lumps out of me in those epic games all those years ago!

An interesting feature of life in our new house was that we acquired a pet. The only pet I can remember having in the family previously was our ill-fated turkey but the least said about that the better! A friend of the family was called Arthur. He was an orphan who visited my Gran's house regularly when she lived in Holywell Street off Marsh Lane, and he continued to visit after the family moved to Netherton. He lived in a flat off Queen's Drive and my cousin and I liked to visit him there. He was an interesting chap with two intriguing hobbies – he was a radio ham and he reared budgerigars both of which we found fascinating. He would crank up his radio set and we would listen in fascination as he talked to fellow enthusiasts in countries across the world or he would tune into shipping or aircraft communications. In the garden of his building he had a shed where he bred his budgerigars. I had persuaded my family that we should have one of his birds and one Sunday he showed me a small nest containing a few eggs. "Pick which one you want" Arthur said and then marked it. A couple of weeks later I saw our bird as a tiny chick and then not long after I took it home in a cardboard box, holding it carefully on the bus ride back to Netherton. My Dad had prepared a cage on a stand and the bird was introduced to its new home. "What shall we call it?" Dad asked. Looking at its beautiful light blue feathers my sister answered "Bluey". It was a remarkable bird and was loved particularly by my sister and Mum. They taught it to talk, and it repeated their phrases as if it was a tape recorder. It even repeated jingles from the advertisements it heard on the TV and radio. Bluey performed all sorts of tricks like riding around on a carriage on my train set or playing dead and rolling over when prompted by my sister. It used to drive my brother mad by picking up his car keys and hiding them. Sadly, after a number of years Bluey flew after Mum when she opened the back door and disappeared. We were all upset but my sister was distraught and late into the night she and her boyfriend Kenny walked the streets with Bluey's cage, calling his name and trying to entice him to return but to no avail. Bluey was never seen again.

Chapter Fifteen Secondary School.

"All hail Salesian school to thee"

First Form Photo at St. Martin's. I am second from the right on the middle row.

When we moved to Netherton I had already started my secondary education at the Salesian College, housed temporarily in St. Martin's on Stanley Road. A remarkable coincidence is that my Dad was a pioneer at St. Martin's when it opened as a secondary school in 1925. He had won a scholarship in those days when most children did not attend secondary school and his Mum, who had a great ambition for him to pursue a professional career, was very proud. However, his Dad, a dock gateman and ex-merchant seaman, had other ideas and he turned up at school one day to take my Dad to Liverpool docks where he had signed him up to the crew of a merchant vessel. That was it and for the next several months he was off sailing to America, all this was without his Mum's knowledge, and she did not speak to my grandfather for a long time. My Dad was fourteen years old. In June 1964 I had received the letter confirming that I had passed the 11 Plus examination and so gained my place at grammar school. To my recollection only four boys from my school had passed and one of them was bound for St. Mary's. My friend Steve has written an excellent account of our school experience at the Salesian entitled "Non Scholae Sed Vitae" (the school motto, Not for School but for Life) and I am indebted to him and my other friends Paul, John, and Jim, who all contributed to the book, for many of the memories shared here. Most of my friends in the street had failed to pass the 11 Plus and indeed the whole invidious system was designed to ensure this outcome. The boys were destined for St. Joan's school and the girls for St. James' senior girls' school. St. Martin's was a fair distance from our street and Dad decided that I would cycle to school. So, on that memorable day on the 8th.of September 1964 I set off in my new blue blazer and uniform proudly wearing long trousers with a leather satchel on my back peddling my older brother's bike. I made my way up Marsh Lane enduring the jeers from the boys on the way to St. Joan's and as I reached Miller's Bridge I fell off the bike, which was much too big for me, ripping my trousers at the knee. It was not the best way to arrive at my new school where I was welcomed at the gate by Father Bowman a kindly Irish priest. I need not have worried, however, as I was beginning what would turn out to be seven very happy years at the school. It was clear from the start that the Salesians were very different to the priests I had known before. They were friendly, enthusiastic about teaching, they liked children but most of all they loved sport, especially football. We were amazed when they joined in the game that began on the schoolyard and it was obvious that they could play a bit. That game played before school, at breaks and lunch times and often after school became a permanent feature of school life and the priests enjoyed it as much as we did. Over the years they demonstrated that they had a love for all sports, and we were encouraged to play cricket, basketball, athletics and even fencing and shinty. The latter was an ancient game popular in the highlands of Scotland. Played with wooden sticks and a wooden ball, it was a sort of violent field hockey with very few rules and injuries were common. The priests were just as keen on this game as we were and on one famous occasion one of the boys smashed his stick in the headmaster's face breaking his glasses and forcing him to attend the hospital casualty unit. We waited for his return with trepidation imagining what steps he would take to exact vengeance as he did have a fearsome reputation. To his credit he returned to school sporting black eyes and bruising, with his glasses held together with tape, never referring to the incident and carrying on teaching and playing shinty as if nothing had happened. It felt very special to be a pioneer of just 72 pupils and I really enjoyed school life. I made friends on day one and to this day four other pioneers remain my close friends over 50 years later. Lessons were very different to primary school even though there was still an over reliance on didactic teaching and rote learning, but it was a change to be learning French, German and Latin and I particularly enjoyed the practical Science lessons. My mate Sully and I particularly looked forward to the Chemistry lessons when acid would be used. We played a game of dare putting a finger into the flask of acid and seeing who would "chicken out" by pulling their finger out first!

The Salesians had a great reputation for training boys in technical skills in Italy, the country where the order was founded. They tried to introduce elements of this into our curriculum with subjects like Engineering Process and Design and Technical Drawing, but I found those practical subjects not really to my taste. All I recall is drilling holes in a strip of metal which was meant to be a drill gauge but mine turned out to be pretty useless. On one memorable occasion the teacher in the workshop had asked me to saw a large piece of plywood in two. "Even you should manage that Rourke!" he said clearly not impressed with my practical skills. He set it up for me on several work stools and I knelt on top of the sheet and began sawing away. I found it really difficult and was struggling when he came to check on my progress. "What are you doing? You should well have finished by now," he said only to discover that not only had I cut through the plywood but also neatly sawed a work stool in two. Needless to say, he did not ask me to do very much after that and to this day I find it difficult to saw a piece of wood in a straight line. No matter how good relations were between the boys and most of the staff they did not shirk from the use of corporal punishment when they felt it necessary. A favoured device was the Bunsen burner tube, a hard plastic pipe which could leave a deep impression on the backside and make it painful to sit down. An alternative was the leather strap which again could bring tears to the eyes no matter how indifferent to the pain you were trying your best to appear in front of your colleagues. The strange thing is that there was never any rancour in this, and punishments were metered out and accepted as part of the normal practice of school life with little bad feeling on any side. In fact, the teacher who had strapped you minutes before might well be playing alongside you in the lunchtime football game or coaching you in a practice session for a school match on Saturday morning. I did think I was in danger of a really serious punishment after we had moved to the new school in Netherton. During a maths lesson I gave a silly answer to a question asked by the teacher. I was embarrassed as laughter rang out and shortly afterwards a note was passed to me from a boy sitting in a desk opposite to mine. This individual had been needling me on several occasions, for reasons best known to himself, so I was really angry when I opened the note to read "Rourke you are as thick as pig dung" although he had used a different word and he made a disgusting reference to a girl I was dating at the time. Incensed and not even thinking about it I threw a punch at him and the next second we were rolling round the classroom floor trying to kill one another. The teacher calmly walked across and dragged us to our feet. As I stood panting facing my opponent two thoughts went through my head. The first was that it was a pity the fight was stopped because for once I had the upper hand and it may have resulted in only the second victory I had ever secured. The second thought was that I was in big trouble and that my punishment would at least be six of the best or, worse, a suspension because this could not be kept hidden from my parents. I need not have worried, however, because the teacher, Father Hughes, was a wise man and not one to overreact. Not wishing to over complicate matters he did not enquire as to the reason for the fight. He simply made us apologise, shake hands and we returned to our desks and got on with our maths work as if nothing had happened.

Life at St. Martin's was very enjoyable, and we were comfortable in the building despite its somewhat run-down state and its outside toilets. It was a redbrick building with a haphazard layout for a school. In the first year my classroom was below ground level and it was heated by a roaring coal fire on one side of the room. In the second year we were joined by a new cohort of pupils and the accommodation began to become stretched and overcrowded. We were anticipating with eagerness the move to the newly built school on Netherton Way. By now I was living in Netherton and travelling to Stanley Road on the 28 bus but after the move I would be able to walk to school. We moved to the new site in September 1966 and you could not fail to be impressed with the facilities we now had at our disposal. The site boasted a science and technology block with state-of-the-art laboratories and workshops, modern bright classrooms, a library, lecture theatre, large hall, a gymnasium and changing rooms with individual showers. Best of all we had large playing fields with superb football pitches and a pristine cricket square which was roped off and cared for by the priests themselves. It was a capital offence to set foot on the cricket square and we all knew this. The school also boasted a chapel and an accommodation building for the priests connected to the school by a glazed corridor. There were priests retired from teaching living there and carrying out various community duties. Sadly, one of them passed away one time and arrangements were made for his funeral to take place in the school. The day before his funeral service he was brought to the chapel and laid in an open coffin. Altar boys were tasked to watch over him in twos for an hour at a time. As there were not enough altar boys to fill the schedule volunteers were asked for. My friend Sully stunned me by suggesting that we volunteer. I was not keen until he pointed out that we would miss lessons for an hour. So for the only time in my life, I donned altar boy clothes and one of the priests instructed us in our duties which was to kneel and pray beside the coffin. As he left, we looked like heavenly angels with our hands clasped, praying fervently. After he had gone Sully opened his eyes, sat on the altar steps and then produced a deck of cards from under his cassock. He spent the next hour teaching me how to play stud poker as we kept a watchful eye out for the teacher's return so we could quickly resume our saintly poses! I don't think we consciously meant any disrespect. The priest, in fact, had been a kindly, friendly man, but I would like to think that he would have been more interested in our card game than the whispered prayers we were meant to say. The chapel featured in further memorable episodes and two in particular spring to mind, one humorous and the other less so. One Good Friday I decided to attend the special mass being held in the school. On this most solemn of occasions the mass was to be a concelebration with five priests officiating and numerous altar boys. The mass proceeded smoothly until one of the small altar boys began to sway and then vomited spectacularly all over the altar steps. It was hard to maintain the solemn, serious demeanour required but the priests and most of the congregation just about managed it. One of the priests whispered into the ear of one of the older altar boys who exited only to return shortly after carrying a mop and pail of soapy water. Unfortunately, he slipped on some of the mess on the altar steps and fell head over heels showering the priests and altar boys with water. This time no one could contain themselves and stifled laughter broke out everywhere. It was some time before normal service was resumed. A couple of years later I decided to attend midnight mass on Christmas Eve at the school. I had taken my girlfriend for a few drinks in the Mons Hotel in Bootle, and we caught the 56 bus home. As there was a bus stop right outside Denise's house, I thought it safe enough to leave her and I got off the bus on Netherton Way. I was dressed warmly in a suit and a Crombie overcoat, and it was a little stuffy in the chapel. I began to feel awful and for the first time in my life I fainted. I must have been carried out because the next thing I was conscious of was coming round as I lay on the ground looking at the streetlights on Netherton Way. Then I looked up to find our eccentric head teacher Father Gordon standing over me pointing his finger threateningly and saying "How dare you come to mass drunk. You are an absolute disgrace. Report to my office first thing on the sixth of January!" In fact, I had only had two pints of beer over the whole evening, it was all I could afford but Father Gordon could not be persuaded that I was the innocent victim of a fainting spell. In fact, I was to faint on two more occasions both times while attending mass in my local church, Our Lady of Walsingham. I can only imagine that I was being sent a message from on high that I was not welcome!

As far as I was concerned the best part of school life was the importance the school placed on sport and particularly football in my case. One of our first fixtures was against the young boys training for the priesthood at Shrigley Park near Macclesfield. I was in the second eleven for this game and we imagined that we would easily triumph over boys training for the religious life. How wrong we were. Our opponents stunned us when just before the game they stood in a circle and said a prayer. This struck me as distinctly unsporting as, after all, we had not asked for divine assistance. It turned out that most of the boys came from working class areas of Scotland and my midfield opposite number at the start of the game said to me "Let's make it England versus Scotland!" in a menacing Glaswegian snarl and then proceeded to try and kick me off the park. I would like to think that I was not the wimpy Sassenach he imagined me to be and that I gave him as good as I got, particularly as I remembered my Dad's advice to clatter my opposite number at the earliest opportunity. True enough they played like it was the final of the World Cup and finished the game as worthy winners, though they did us proud with the pie and pea lunch their canteen served up. We returned to Netherton with our tails between our legs but wiser and determined that when they came to Netherton Way for the return fixture they would face a sterner test. It was not all doom and gloom, however, because I must have shown enough in the game to be promoted to the first eleven where I soon became captain and kept my place for the next six years. Being in the team gave you status in the school and respect from pupils and staff. Teams were announced at assembly before the weekend and before important games we would get time out of class for extra practise. Games were usually played in the Merseyside block fixtures on Saturday mornings and for away games this meant coach journeys up Queen's Drive or to Kirkby or Huyton and so we became familiar with large areas of Merseyside. I recall those early Saturday mornings with fond memories, the sun coming up on a misty or frosty morning and the sheer delight and anticipation of lining up in pristine kit on a field of green before battle commenced. Games were very rarely postponed, and I can remember playing in thick fog, on frozen pitches which were as hard as iron and sometimes on fields that resembled shallow lakes. On one occasion we had to drag our boots through thick snow to mark out the lines on the pitch and then played the game in a blizzard. Our team improved gradually, and we began to hold our own against some of the strongest schools on Merseyside – S.F.X, De La Salle and St. Kevin's – schools that fielded future professionals and England internationals. One indication of how seriously the teachers regarded their duties as coaches was the fact that they wrote detailed match reports which were posted on the notice board on Mondays and were eagerly consumed. On one occasion we had secured a rare victory away against S.F.X. scoring a first half goal and then defending stoutly in the second half. In fact, the report on the following Monday gave me my school nickname. Father Lavery had written in his report that, "Rourke played like a brick in defence." That was it – from being known simply as "Rourkie" I became "Brick" for the rest of my school life. At least that is my version. Less generous ex-colleagues have snidely commented that the nickname originated from the observation "as thick as a brick," but I stand by my story. Years later at the wedding of my school friend John's daughter I met his younger brother, who had also attended the school, for the first time since leaving. "Why it's Brick," he remarked when he saw me. I replied, "That's the first time anyone has called me that in over 40 years." Of course, one of the benefits of playing early Saturday mornings is that there was ample time to travel to Goodison Park for the game kicking off at 03:00 pm. In fact the weekend was a feast of football as on Saturday evenings it would be a Subbuteo tournament at Stenno's house, a friend even though he was a Kopite, followed by "Match of the Day" and then the all afternoon football match on the school field on Sunday.

Chapter Sixteen Teenage Social Life

"I got Friday on my mind"

Another great feature of the new school was that it had a youth centre on the ground floor of the community building. This was a forward-thinking initiative on behalf of the Salesians. The Don Bosco Youth Club was run by Fr. De Bono who came from Malta and seemed very exotic to our eyes and certainly had a Mediterranean charm which impressed the girls in the club. The club was a haven, somewhere for teenagers to go in a desert of leisure provision. It was open to anyone and so was a great opportunity to make wider acquaintances and, of course, a chance, for boys attending a single sex school, to meet girls. There were pool tables and various games, and I was taught to play table tennis by two girls who it turned out were friends with my future wife. In fact, Denise came to the club a few times, probably when I was there, but I do not think she thought it was cool enough for her and her "Mod" friends. Despite this for me the club was an introduction to teenage culture and fashion. "Mod" culture, which had begun in London in the early 1960s, was still prevalent for a few years and there were boys and girls who set the trend for everyone

192

else. The club had a good sound system, and it was there that I discovered Soul music. Before that all I knew was the popular stuff by the Beatles, Herman's Hermits and the other acts dominating the charts but one evening a group of girls from St. Catherine's school arrived with their record collection and soon the Four Tops, the Temptations and Otis Redding were blasting out of the speakers. I was an instant convert and, like most switched on teenagers in Liverpool, considered the music of our own Beatles as fine for our parents or younger brothers and sisters while we preferred the music coming from Motown and Atlanta. A great feature of the club was the monthly dance. Tickets sold out quickly and they featured live bands as well as DJ music. A popular act was "Nolan's Feelings" fronted by the brother of one of our classmates. Unlike today, teenagers really dressed up for nights out and the dance was no exception. The girls looked amazing in their mod gear and haircuts and lads wore suits and jackets and ties. It was for the dances that I purchased my first suit and, as was the custom then, this was a "made to measure" from Burton's on London Road in Liverpool where, with much deliberation, material was chosen from a book of samples, and this was followed by a choice of lining. The next step was the style of suit which involved decisions about the collar, size of collar, length of jacket, number of buttons, one or two vents and size of vent and so on.

It was a very complicated business and after all that the measuring began. Two follow up visit were needed for fittings before the suit was finally ready. A far cry from picking a suit off the peg, which is the norm now, but you felt like a film star when you wore your suit for the first time and displayed it for the critical acclaim of the very discerning participants at the dance. The dances were a unique opportunity to meet girls and get up close in the "slowies". The priests were always on duty but seemed very tolerant of boys and girls getting to know one another in close personal contact. I met my first girl friend at a dance and my second come to that. I took my first girlfriend for a magical day out on the ferry to New Brighton when the sun was shining, and the latest hit "Whiter Shade of Pale" was being played everywhere. Joyce was very pretty with auburn hair, and she caused a sensation one time when she came tripping on to the school field with a friend, both sporting miniskirts, to see me compete in sports day. I was so surprised I almost dropped the shot, which I was preparing to throw, on my foot but the whole episode did not harm my "street cred" one bit. Continuing the nautical theme, I took my second girlfriend on an evening disco cruise on the "Royal Iris" and I tried to impress her by telling her of my experience as a young boy in steering the ship, but I could tell she probably did not believe me. Eventually as I became older, I began to roam further afield and the soul clubs in Liverpool became an irresistible attraction.

A constant topic of conversation at school and amongst friends was the lure of beer and going to the pub. Lads who were lucky enough to look older than their years would brag about being served at the bar and drinking copious (but hardly believable) amounts of beer. The first pint of beer I can remember drinking in a pub was when I attended my cousins wedding in Chorley. My cousin David and my sister's boyfriend Kenny persuaded me to join them in rushing off to a pub near the church as the coach transporting our family from Netherton had arrived early. Despite being only fifteen I must have looked quite the part in my barathea blazer with a military badge on the pocket, all the rage at the time, my cavalry twill trousers and brogue shoes. They bought me a pint of brown mixed, half a bitter with a bottle of Mann's brown added and although I did not like it very much, I felt very grown up as I cautiously sipped it. It cost one shilling and sixpence (or seven and a half pence in the new money). Together with friends from school we began to visit pubs in Maghull as we thought we had more chance of being served there. Vinny, who looked older than the rest of us, would go to the bar while the rest of us would do our best to look inconspicuous in a corner of the pub. We discovered Double Diamond a popular light ale which suited our taste better than the stronger flavoured bitters and milds. Some pubs were just beginning to stock lagers like Carling Black Label and Skol which we liked although my Dad scathingly referred to it as "onion ale" and he remembered drinking it abroad on his sea voyages. Usually, we could only afford one pint each which we tried to make last as long as possible and then we faced a long walk back to Netherton as we had no money left for the train fare.

My friends Vinny, Stenno and myself were keen want to be mods and we did our best to keep up with the latest fashions, although our lack of adequate finance was always a limit on our ambitions. One of Vinny's older brothers had a group of friends that we took a lead from and tried to emulate. Like them we began to visit Eric's store in Lime Street to check out what was on offer, and we tried to dress like our role models. Colourful Ben Sherman shirts were essential although a blue or green Jaytex shirt was an acceptable alternative or if you wanted to be more casual a Fred Perry polo shirt. Levi jeans were popular, although I always preferred Lee Riders and many favoured Fleming's jeans which were made in Liverpool. The advantage of Fleming's was that you could visit the shop and have a pair made to measure. Brogue leather soled shoes or "comos" completed the look. We thought we looked the business and felt appropriately dressed to take our place at the Litherland Fair or the annual fair held on the

Littlewoods' sports field off Park Lane. These were splendid summer occasions frequented from all the young people in the area and they were a good opportunity to be seen and to meet new people. The coloured lights and loud music coming from the fairground rides made for a magical atmosphere although we boys were always resentful of the attention the girls gave to the young men working on the rides, who we considered to be dubious characters, who would show off as they spun the "waltzes" and flirted shamelessly with the girls. Occasionally there would be trouble between rival gangs, and I can remember one evening when fighting broke out at the Litherland fair between a gang from Marsh Lane and one from "Dodge". It resembled a medieval pitched battle and my friends and I carefully made a discreet exit and left them to it. It was at Litherland fair that I first met my future wife. Denise was a year older than I and hung out with an older crowd most of whom had left school and had jobs and hence money and so seemed out of our league. But one of her friends was attracted to my friend Vinny and I suppose she was keen for us all to meet up and I paired off with Denise. We dated for a few weeks, but she then told me she wanted to split up and, although this was a blow to my pride, I took it in my stride as the "knock back" or "k.b." as we called it then was part of the game and had to be accepted if you wanted to participate. I suspect the fact that I was a "schoolie" (I had joined the Sixth Form) and a year younger was partly behind her decision as her friends dated older boys with jobs and money. However, I was surprised a few weeks later to receive a letter from her. In these days of instant communication by text or mobile phone it is difficult to recall the significance of receiving a letter but in fact, as we had no telephone, this was the only way of communicating with me. Needless to say, the rest is history and apparently it was Denise's Mum and younger sister Karen who had persuaded her to change her mind as they had taken a shine to me.

Despite the distractions of football, fairs, and youth club I had done surprisingly well in my "O" levels and entered the Sixth Form to study "A" levels in English Literature, History, Economics and General Studies. I was to enjoy the next two years as much as my previous years in the school. In the Sixth Form we were divided into an Arts class and a Science class or "Boffins" as we called them with derision as we thought they were pretty unsophisticated, after all several of them were Kopites. I am not sure what they called us. We were a select group of just seven and five of us were Bluenoses and are still firm friends to this day. Our classroom was a sectioned off part of a corridor right next to the staff room and teachers were always passing through. In the Sixth Form we wore black blazers and as I was Head Boy and my friend

Steve Deputy Head Boy, our blazers had the addition of a silver stripe. I am not sure why I was chosen as Head Boy as in my school career I could not claim an unblemished disciplinary record and I had had my share of whacks with the Bunsen burner pipe and strap. Cynics would say it was because my Dad was Chair of the P.T.A. but I would prefer to think that it was because I was captain of the school football team. Life in the Sixth Form was very pleasant, and I enjoyed the lessons even though the work could be hard with lots of homework to follow but there was still a lot of time to devote to football practice and preparing for school matches at the weekend. Through our shared interest in Everton there was a nonstop conversation about football and anticipation for the games that were coming up. We were fortunate in that this was a golden period in our club's fortunes and the dominance of our great rivals was still in the future. One popular diversion was our invention of a tabletop football game which was a form of shove ha'penny. In his book "NSSV" Steve gives a detailed history of this game and indeed of our time in the Sixth Form and describes better than I can the passion and importance that this simple game assumed in our school life. It was great fun and I often wonder what the teachers in the staffroom next door must have thought when they heard the groans and shouts of celebration that emanated from our room. Certainly, none of them ever remarked on the fact that one of the tables in our room was now marked out with the traditional lines of a miniature football pitch. A couple of years later in August I phoned the school to find out the results of my examinations. Not expecting much I had not bothered to go into school on results day, but I was surprised to find that I had done well and more than achieved the offer grades to gain a place at university to study economic history. This meant a change in plan as I also had the offer to begin a trainee manager's job with the Higson's brewery. I often wonder how different my life might have been if I had revised a little less.

My social life at this time began to develop as my horizons broadened and the bright lights of the city were an irresistible attraction. The mod era was slowly coming to an end, but soul music was still the choice of the in crowd of young people in Liverpool. Popular venues were the "Mardi Gras" club and the "Victoriana". The "Mardie" as it was affectionately known was in Mount Pleasant Street and had been a chapel but opened as a beat and jazz club in !957. It had two floors with a stage and dance floor, two bars and a snack bar. The upstairs bar was located at the rear of a grand balcony which provided a splendid bird's eye view of the dance floor and stage. The lighting featured ultraviolet lights which made white clothing glow which embarrassed unwary girls whose underclothes would be picked out splendidly through their dresses. It also played tricks with capped teeth and fillings, and more than a few dancers sported dazzling mouths. It was a members' only club for over 18s, but it was not difficult to obtain a membership card and my girlfriend, friends and I all had one. It had become a soul venue and the resident DJ was Billy Butler, an enthusiastic champion of the genre, who became a co- owner of the club. The Mardi Gras was popular with black teenagers, and they made up a fair proportion of the clientele at a time when most clubs were virtually all white. At the weekend it featured live acts and many of them were from the USA. We saw some fabulous performers like Chairman of the Board, the Drifters, Charles and Inex Foxx, Jimmy Ruffin, the Show Stoppers and my particular favourites Johnny Johnson and the Bandwagon. In those days performers dressed in smart suits and had dance routines to accompany their singing and they really put on a show. The sister club to the Mardi Gras was the Victoriana and the live acts performed at both venues, so you had the opportunity to see your favourite acts twice if you timed it right. It was not only the performers who dressed up as most of the boys wore suits or smart jackets. The girls looked splendid in their mod dresses or blouses and skirts and clubs had cloakrooms as most people wore coats and overcoats in the cold weather and they could be checked in for a small fee in return for a small draw ticket to reclaim them later. I became the proud owner of a "Crombie" overcoat which I felt really smart in particularly when complemented with a paisley scarf and black leather gloves. Now young people venture forth in the rain and snow on a night out looking as if they are dressed for a summer evening on the Strip in Magaluf. The Mardi Gras was demolished in 1975 as part of the plan to bring the M62 into the city centre, a plan which never materialised. Smokie Mo's a popular American themed bar now occupies the site. The Victoriana was a popular soul venue for young people, and it seemed a little more upmarket than the Mardi Gras but featured the same type of music and live acts and was a top venue for a night out. Although many great performers could be seen in the more intimate atmosphere of the clubs, the really big stars could only be seen at the larger venues like Liverpool University, Liverpool Stadium, and the Empire. We saw some great performers like the Four Tops and the Temptations at the Empire and as musical tastes began to shift, the Who, again at the Empire where they destroyed their set at the end of the concert to the bemusement of most of the audience. My future brother-in-law Kenny who had a more eclectic music taste than most of us took us to see Status Quo at Liverpool Stadium – I'm not sure if my hearing has ever recovered – Wizzard and Lou Reed and the Velvet Underground at Liverpool University.

Towards the end of the Sixties and into the seventies fashions and musical tastes had slowly changed. Hard rock became popular and the music in the clubs followed suit The Babalou Club in Seel Street was very popular, and many clubbers began to dress more casually which reflected the stage wear of some of the popular rock groups. Some clubbers still wore suits, but lapels and ties became wider, and flares became a necessary fashion item. We were about to enter the very different world of the '70s.

Chapter Seventeen Work and Transport

"I can't do what ten people tell me to do"

This was a very vibrant and busy time for me juggling schoolwork with my sporting interests and social life. To facilitate my life at that time I felt I needed two things – transport and money. The money came from a series of holiday jobs, but the transport arrived in the form of a blue Vespa scooter. When I mentioned my need for a more efficient form of transport than my old bike my Dad said he would sort it. He knew of my admiration for the Mod style of transport in the form of Italian scooters and in fact my brother-in-law had recently purchased a beautiful red Lambretta. One evening my Dad and Kenny went off and shortly after Kenny returned driving a very tired looking Vespa which he claimed had been a death trap to ride with its very worn tyres, both of which sported serious looking eggs. My Dad sensing my disappointment told me not to be concerned as he would soon have it looking spick and span. After a few days of replacing parts and a paint job my Dad declared it ready. It certainly looked better and sounded better as he kicked the engine over. "Right," he said brightly "on you get." I was not at all sure as I had never driven a mechanical mode of transport in

204

my life, but Dad would not take no for an answer. "Nothing to it," he declared as he gave me the briefest of instructions. This was outside our house in the close with everyone looking on with interest. I climbed on, clicked it in to gear as instructed but then twisted the accelerator too heavily and let out the clutch too quickly. The scooter roared off across the close with Kenny and my Dad desperately trying to halt my progress by grabbing the seat but to no avail. The scooter shot across the close narrowly avoiding some panicked onlookers and smashed straight into the front garden gate of our neighbour destroying it in the process. Needless to say, it was sometime later, after Dad had repaired the scooter once again and replaced our neighbour's gate, that I remounted the Vespa this time on the road and after more measured and detailed instruction. However, I have to say that there were a few more hairy moments waiting for me in the future riding that scooter, but it did open up my horizons. It meant I could ride over to my girlfriend's Denise's house and return home without relying on the 56 bus. We could also go for trips out and it is amazing to think that her Mum and Dad, usually so sensible, allowed her to ride pillion without even the protection of a helmet. In fact, strictly speaking I should not have been carrying passengers at all as I only had a provisional licence but on Sunday, I would take off the learner plates and we would ride down to my newly married sister's flat in St. Catherine's Road

Bootle to spend the evening. One evening we arrived back on the bus from town after seeing the Who in concert. When it was time for me to go home, I stripped the plastic sheet off the scooter, which I used to keep it dry as it was parked in Denise's front garden, only to find that like a magic trick it had disappeared. Denise's Mum was mortified to realise that it had been pinched literally from under her nose as she watched television. When I went to report it missing the next day at Copy Lane police station, the desk sergeant, after a few phone calls, informed me that the scooter was safely parked outside Seaforth police station. To be fair whoever had stolen it had only wanted it to get home. After a while the kick start on the scooter failed to work and the only way I could get it to start was to push it quickly, jam it in gear and then jump on as it took off – a risky business but highly amusing for onlookers. Eventually after I purchased my first car, I sold the scooter to my friend Paul for the princely sum of £2, with a helmet thrown in. To this day he claims to have been robbed and he has never forgiven me for the humiliation he had to endure when he took the scooter for an M.O.T. test. The mechanics fell about in hysterics and did not charge him because they said it had given them such a laugh. Needless to say, this did not give him much comfort as he pushed the worthless machine home! I still feel bad about this and one day I am determined to return his £2.

It is hard to imagine it now, but it was very easy to secure temporary jobs during the holidays when at school and later at university. Jobs were plentiful and it was possible to leave one you did not particularly like on a Friday and start another on Monday. The first job I had was at Parr's Wood Yard on Dunnings Bridge Road near to the Park Hotel. My friend Les, who was an apprentice there, got me the job for the summer holidays when I was 15. At that time, you could leave school at that age although I was staying on a year to complete my "O" levels. It was quite a change from school with its longer working day and being amongst many older adults. The job consisted of standing at the end of a mechanical saw and stacking the wood neatly in a pile as the machinist cut it to order. There was little regard for health and safety and despite the loud screeching noise as the wood passed through the machine, ear defenders were not a requirement and in fact I did not see any evidence of them. At night, falling to sleep, the sound of the machine still rang in my ears. On my first day my Mum had given me a pair of gloves to protect my hands much to the amusement of the regular workers. By lunchtime they were worn through and totally useless and I just had to put up with the splinters and wait for my hands to toughen up. It was satisfying to see the pile of wood on the machinist's side fall lower and lower until the last piece was put through the machine but there was no respite as this was just the signal for a forklift truck to immediately drop off the next load. My wages were the princely sum of £4, 19 shillings and 11 pence but this could be boosted by almost another pound by working overtime on Saturday morning. Another way to increase your pay was to be willing to go into "the box". This was a huge green open topped wooden container which was placed under the extraction pipe that deposited all the saw dust and small wooden particles that had been sucked up from all the machines. This was taken away by a firm that produced hardboard. Your job in the box was to shovel the deposits to the corners of the box to ensure an even spread to fill up the box. It was an extremely dusty job, again with no protective equipment, and you ended up covered in the stuff from head to foot and it had to be shaken out of your clothes and underpants in the evening. As the box began to fill up you rose higher and higher until you had filled the whole container and this process could take up to three days. The machinists thought it amusing to slip larger chunks of wood in the suction pipes hoping to hear a howl from the poor wretch in the box as the wood hit his head. There was an upside to being in the box however as the contractor would give you a generous tip, when he came to collect the container, if you had filled the box correctly. One time I was tipped a fiver which doubled my weekly pay which was a very welcome surprise. The following summer my sister managed to get me and my mate Shorty a summer job in Lunt's Soap factory off Park Lane. This was easy to spot as it had a large brick chimney with Lunt's emblazoned on it. It employed many women of all ages who worked on the various production lines. Lunt's produced many products including candles, industrial and household cleaning products and personal cleaning items like bubble bath and soap. To my surprise it produced some expensive luxury products for various well-known firms and the management always reserved the right to search employees when they left the premises. Again, health and safety did not feature prominently, and personal protection was virtually non-existent. One time my sister had an allergic reaction as she worked on the "Noddy Bubble Bath" production line. Her job was to wipe the surplus soap from the containers as they were filled – "Wiping Noddy's bum," was how she prosaically described it. The chemicals in the mix caused her face to swell up horribly and she was ill for days. Many of the production methods had not changed for years and there was a great reliance on manual labour. On one famous occasion the firm invested in a machine to box candles in an attempt to improve efficiency but when it was first trialled it was easily beaten by one of the ladies who had worked in that department for years. I worked for two summers at Lunt's and in the first summer Vinny and I were sent to work in the department making industrial cleaner. This was made from a number of ingredients and heated up in a huge cauldron. When it was ready our job was to stand underneath the boiler and operate the handle on a pipe to fill hundredweight green cans with the boiling liquid cleaner and then stack the cans two high until they cooled, and the cleaner became solid. After that we would hammer on lids and then load the cans on a trolley to a waiting truck where we lifted and stacked them to be taken away. It was extremely hot, thirsty, tiring and now I come to think of it, potentially dangerous work. The heat was such that we worked bare chested even though splashes of the liquid soap could burn your skin. On day one the foreman gave each of us a half gallon flask of lime juice. I said "What's this for? I'll never drink all of that". But I did and on every following day. When I returned home in the evening and took off my work jeans they could stand up straight themselves as they were caked with solidified soap. Another danger of working topless was the attention it drew from some of the female workforce. Some of the older women, some of them the same age as my Mum, used to shout some truly shocking suggestions to us that made me squirm and blush with embarrassment. My mate Vinny made the foolish mistake of trying to verbally spar with them, but he was not in their league and had to run for his life as they chased him fully intending to debag him. This was all a real education for me as, apart from my Gran, the older women in my life had been my Headmistress nuns, my aunties and of course, my Mum whose only expletives were, "Jesus, Mary and Joseph," and "Bejeezus." My second summer at Lunt's was not as traumatic, as I knew what to expect and I was placed in the "Movie" department. This involved making, canning, and shipping what was once a popular and very effective oven cleaner. After a couple of weeks, I actually became the Movie department as the other, permanent, member of the department was sacked for poor time keeping. One of the foremen showed me what to do and left me to it. The process began with filling a tank with water. It was about ten feet high, and I had to stand on a table to add the rest of the ingredients, most of which consisted of sacks of caustic soda, which I had to lift in hundredweight bags, rest them carefully on the edge of the tank, slit them open with a Stanley knife and then pour the contents into the mix. The danger was allowing one of the sacks to fall into the tank as it was a messy job retrieving it but, thankfully, I managed to avoid this most of the time. One or two minor ingredients followed finished off with a blue dye and perfume which were purely for cosmetic purposes. I was surprised at how simple it was to make the cleaner which would have worked just as well without the colouring and the perfume. Then it was a case of switching on the rotating blade to stir the mix, heating it and bringing it up to the required temperature. This was critical as if too cold the

211

ingredients did not mix properly and if too hot the resulting cleaner became mottled in appearance. As this process could take several hours it was easy to have a "sit off," (an easy time) and pretend to look busy and important by frequently checking the temperature with a thermometer fixed to a piece of string. This could not be stretched out too long, unfortunately, as the liquid cleaner had to be canned while at the correct heat. Canning was a pleasant task also as the cans were only small and could be stacked to cool on the large table next to the boiler. They had to be left for a while to cool and again it was easy to look busy while waiting for this and to appear as if preparing for the next batch. This involved visiting other parts of the factory to collect bags of materials and it was a good opportunity to chat to people. As long as I had the cans ready for delivery at the right time the foreman did not bother me. The final task was to put the lids on and fix the labels on the tins and then box them, again not taxing work. On only one occasion was my peaceful existence in the Movie department troubled when a foreman came in with a disgruntled supplier. It appears that when he came in to pick up his delivery of boxes of oven cleaner he was outraged. "I'm not being fobbed off with that Movie," he stormed "it's rubbish!" The foreman tried to placate him and said there had been a mix up which he would sort out and took him to the office for coffee while he waited for us to find his proper order.

I was very confused and when the foreman returned, he explained the problem. He said that the supplier ordered "Blitzo" oven cleaner which he considered to be far superior to Movie. "But we only make one oven cleaner, Movie," I pointed out, "who makes Blitzo?" "We do," he replied and gave me a box with Blitzo labels in and instructed me to remove all the Movie labels from the consignment and replace them with Blitzo labels as fast as I could. The supplier left happy, consoled by the fact that he now had the oven cleaner which he knew to be the best. I had learnt an important lesson in product differentiation and consumer choice! I thoroughly enjoyed my second summer at Lunt's as it was far less physically demanding than the job I had the previous summer and I left with a feeling of affection for Movie, the virtues of which I was always keen to extol to anyone who would listen, and it saddened me to discover a few years later that it was no longer produced. In the days before I left one of the foremen had a word with me and said that I had done a good job and he offered me a permanent position saying, "You could become a foreman in a few years." But a return to Sixth Form to complete my "A" levels was my destiny, something which I do not think he considered was the better option.

In my final year in the Sixth Form, I managed to get two weeks work in the Easter holiday at the tax office in Bootle. This was something of a risk as I should have been studying flat out for my final examinations but the need for finance was strong and I managed to take the job and squeeze my revision in at the same time. The tax office was in Merton Road and for the first time I went to work in a shirt and tie but, for the work they gave me, I should have worn a boiler suit. In those days all the tax records were paper based and kept in cardboard wallet files which were kept in wooden shelving units which covered a large part of the office space. Tax officers sat at desks dealing with correspondence and they requested files and had copies of the various letters and forms to be filed. This was the job of clerical assistants who collected the files and returned them to the shelves, a task which was called linking and sorting. It was not as easy as it sounds as the files were often bulging and sometimes bursting apart and it took some effort to pull them from the crammed shelves and even more effort to push them back into place. You would see people literally hammering on the files to drive them back into their place on the shelf and, as the files were very dusty, it could be a messy business. The system was a little chaotic and prone to mistakes. Letters and forms would spill out of files and often these would end up on the floor and behind the shelves. Occasionally they would be swept up and placed in a large cardboard box. This is where I came in. Arriving on my first day I was introduced to a huge box containing hundreds of bits of dusty paper and my task was to return each piece to its correct file using the name on the document or its reference number. It was an extremely boring, repetitive, and dusty task and the pile of papers never seemed to grow any smaller. If you were ever frustrated with dealings with your tax issues in those days, it is possible that some of your vital correspondence lay under the shelves or in a big brown box waiting for a student employee to find it a home in the term time holidays. There was some respite from the drudgery, however, as each time the HEO (Higher Executive Officer), who over saw the office, left his desk then all work would immediately stop, and everyone would have a break to have a chat or read the paper or even take out their knitting. On several occasions I was made to sit beside a desk and hold both hands out as one of the ladies wound her wool. Another diversion to look forward to was half way through the morning and then afternoon as we all listened out for the rattling of the arrival of the tea and cake trolley when we would queue up for a welcome break. The final action of the day was in the few minutes before five o'clock as everyone began to surreptitiously slip on their coat and glance at their watch. Eventually the HEO would look up, look at his watch and call out "Good Evening," which was the signal for a mad dash for the exit and hopefully, a charge to Stanley Road in time to catch a bus home. I surmised that this was the white-collar version of the clocking off that I was more accustomed to.

Epilogue

I was to have other jobs in the future: in Vernon's Catalogues on Hawthorne Road carrying bags of catalogues – the only job I have ever been fired from for going to the pub with my mate Paul during the afternoon break; with Liverpool Warehouse Company when I witnessed our warehouse being gutted by fire and where I became infested with fleas; and finally with the Ribble Bus company working as a conductor or "guard" as it was called where I quickly realised that the unofficial mission statement was "Pick up as few passengers as possible."; but this was all in the future and the !970s. The new decade was an eventful time for me. My father died while on holiday just a few days after taking early retirement and weeks before my "A" level results. I think he would have been proud to know that I had gained a place at university. I was to venture abroad for the first time, start university, become engaged and then married and begin a long and eventful career in teaching – but all that is another story.

As I look back now on my early years of growing up in Bootle in the '50s and '60s I remember that time with a great fondness and very few regrets. Life seemed a lot simpler in those days: working people like ourselves voted Labour and valued and trusted our politicians and the trade union movement which had done so much to improve the lives of so many; you knew that to get on and be successful you had to work hard and get a good job unlike today when some lucky young people, who seem to have nothing more to offer other than good looks, can feature in some ridiculous reality television programme and then earn a fortune as an "influencer" whatever that might be; celebrities were famous and popular for having a particular talent unlike now when many so called "celebrities" seem to have no notable attributes that I can discern; when you purchased a product all you needed to know to be certain that you had bought a quality item was to see the "made in Britain" label or the BSI (British Standard Institute) kite mark; banks and companies valued their customers and rewarded them for their loyalty unlike today when those who remain with an organisation are regarded as fair game and face hiked up charges each year; everyone paid their taxes and those who were better off paid more on a progressive scale unlike today when the rich do everything they can to avoid paying tax, if they pay anything at all, all the while extolling the virtues of this country and its institutions; you knew all the names of the footballers, many of whom were local lads who would be standing with you on the terraces if they had not made it as a professional and players lived in our world, in ordinary houses and drove ordinary cars and certainly did not travel in private executive jets; football fans were overwhelmingly working class in those days before the Premier League came along, football became fashionable and rich people, politicians and celebrities suddenly realised that they had been supporters of a particular football club all their lives after all; comedians were funny, told jokes and made you laugh, a skill many so called modern stand up alternative comedians are sadly lacking in; choosing a television programme was far more straight forward with limited choice and everyone watched at the same time and people would discuss plot lines in work or school; at the cinema everyone watched the same picture as there was only one screen but you did get two movies with an interval in between even if you did have to move quickly at the end to avoid having to stand for the National Anthem; young people could sit together and while away the hours talking without the need to check their social media content every few minutes; you could have a great night out even if you did nurse a half pint of beer most of the evening because it was all you could afford and there was not the imperative to drink yourself insensible which seems to be the norm now. I may not have had the advantages of coming from a privileged, prosperous background but I did have the enormous benefit of having a loving and supportive family and a group of friends who were loyal and fun to be around and with whom I shared many enjoyable and varied activities. What we lacked in material things we more than made up for with imagination and inventiveness. It was also an exciting time to be growing up with the development of teenage culture and the identity, independence, and sense of self-esteem this gave. Also, education offered a way to break through some of the barriers that had existed in the past and I was fortunate to be offered this opportunity. When I secured my place at university I did so from a borough with the lowest rate of university progression in the country, although I was not conscious of this at the time. All in all, I would not swop my upbringing with the wealthiest old Etonian. Who would have thought that a scruffy little Bootle "Scally" would end up as a head teacher of a large high school in one of the most prosperous neighbourhoods on Merseyside? – certainly not my young ten-year-old self as I swam, perfectly content, near the sewage outlet in the cold and murky waters of the River Mersey.

Resources referred to:

"The Lost Tribe of Everton and Scottie Road" Ken Rogers

"Only the Strong Survived – Remembering the Brutal Boy's Pen at Goodison Park in the 1960s" Paul

McParlan

"NSSV- Volume One" Steve Mahon et al

"The rise and fall of Liverpool sectarianism" Keith Daniel Roberts (Liverpool Doctoral Thesis April 2015)

Bootle Times Past – Present – Future website

Printed in Great Britain
by Amazon

15219302R00129